Seasons Of Faith:

From Paralysis
To Purpose

Jonathan Chamis

A Note from the Author

My father is a man who has lived a life devoted to faith. As a minister, as a father and as a person he has always been defined by such a word. In his daily conversations he speaks of faith and his life demonstrates the love brought forth by it. To his local community, his congregants, his family or anyone standing in line beside him in line at the store; his heart shines a light.

Throughout my life, I have seen his principled heart act with such benevolence that at times it baffles me. Whether he was picking up a hitchhiker on his way to work or on a missionary trip to the Dominican Republic, every step he takes seems to be guided by something most indescribable. And if you'd ask him what it is that guides him he'd could sum it up one word ... "faith."

Such a word is so hard to define let alone understand entirely, my father has always said; one has to live it to know. It is for this reason that the following pages have been written. To walk back, following the footsteps of my father's journey with his faith in an attempt at the insurmountable task of understanding it. It is my belief that words can do no justice to such things as "faith" or "love." But a story... a story can deliver its truth. And so, I will tell you Jack's story, in hopes that you too may feel closer to the answers as I have in finding the definition of faith.

Jonathan Chamis

WHO AM I?

John Kennedy Chamis was born August 11, 1965 in the city of Middletown, Connecticut. Like many states bordering the shores of Ellis Island, Connecticut held a thriving community of immigrants seeking new life in America. His parents, Christos Chamis and Florence Pattavina, were the children of two of these immigrants. Born in Rhode Island, brought over with his father & mother from Patras, Greece, Christos had an extraordinary childhood. As an infant he returned to Greece only to be unable to return to America for 8 years as World War II ravaged Europe. Christos' only way of return to America was as a lonely little boy hitching a ride on a United States Naval ship returning to a New York City port following the conclusion of the war. The brave young Greek grew up to marry his high school sweetheart Florence (commonly known as "Flo") the offspring of a Sicilian plaster craftsmen. Their romance blossomed through the years and when the time was right they married to start a family. Their first child, a daughter; named Christa Chamis after her father. Then a son, James, named after Chris' father before him.

John Kennedy came last, the youngest of the three, and was named after the esteemed John Fitzgerald Kennedy, whose death had shattered the hearts of Americans two years earlier. Chris admits that the idea to pay reverence was out of a politically active mindset in those days, but the name still inspired what he hoped would be a great man someday. Though he is most commonly referred to by his nickname "Jack"; it is a name that has fulfilled the promise of his birthright homage.

Jack grew up in a six family household with his cousins, aunts, uncles, grandparents and his own parents. The house was divided into apartments for each family. It was a lively household with 10 children. While the mothers stayed home to tend to the children, the men worked as construction and factory workers. Chris held a position at the local Pratt and Whitney plant, a major industry for Connecticut at the time. Here he manned a machine he called "a boring little thing" that churned out small metal parts for United States Air Force planes. While he regarded this job as a decent paycheck with good benefits, it wasn't long before he would venture out to become a chef of local fame at State Lunch; a restaurant his father James Chamis had started years earlier on Main Street in Middletown which he recalled as being the happiest of his working days.

The household was a bustling one, the families were tight knit and while the rest of the week was spent on work, Sunday was a day of two traditions in the Chamis three story apartment house; family supper and the Red Sox. After the dinner plates were cleared, the fathers and children would gather around the one television set in the house for Sunday Night Baseball. During the days of the "Great Bambino's Curse", any Red Sox fan will tell you, they were underdogs.

It was for this reason Chris holds his allegiance to the Red Sox to this day, they were the every man's team. They couldn't buy new players, couldn't afford a fancy stadium but they played ball and that's all they could do. In these early days, Jack doesn't recall religion having much of a place within the household. As Italians they were Catholics, but more by tradition than a strong belief, as they weren't church going Catholics.

As time went on, Chris and Flo eventually had enough money to purchase their own home to raise their now budding children. Together they settled on a stretch of road surrounded by forest and homes called Oakcliff Road. A different environment than the bustling apartment in the city, Jack enjoyed the days running around with a neighborhood friend Peter and playing in the woods. During this time Chris had taken sole ownership of the restaurant from his father after leaving Pratt and Whitney Aircraft. Chris continued to operate the small diner called State Lunch. And like many restaurants it was a family affair. The family worked six days a week. "We never made much money off it, enough to get by but you know we really did love every second of it." Chris often reminisces about his time and the relationship with his customers and the community he shared there.

The children went to school during the days but the afternoon and evening was time for work. Christa, a 12 year old hostess. Jack and Jimmy (James) were the five and eight year old busboys and dishwashers. Together Chris and Flo raised their children in the restaurant. "It was really quite exciting for a young boy" Jack recalls, "There were so many interesting characters that would wander into the restaurant, being right on main street, the restaurant became a hub of activity throughout the day.

There were all sorts of interesting regulars who would come around. "Danny the Torch", "Frenchie", "Paul" the dishwasher who was a drug addict and cutter...they all had these nicknames and they all knew my father, they'd come in and never need to order. My father knew exactly what they wanted." Customers were often greeted with signature catch phrases such as "Here comes 'double cheese'!" or "Here comes 'a German Shepard running down the street crying'!" (A hot dog with sauerkraut "to go" with onions).

Jack loved being around the restaurant as a kid. All the different people he would meet and the distinct encounters that would happen. He recalls exploring the city with his brother Jimmy.

"Being around ten years old at the time it was very exciting for us, one time I remember we saw a bank robbery...the guy was running down the street with a cop chasing him and the cop tripped, fell and lost his gun. We were stunned. It was like a scene right out of a movie." Early revelations of the more nefarious world of the surrounding downtown streets became more apparent, such as seeing his first porno magazine at a local head shop called "The Devils Den" or Danny The Torch inviting him to come explore some abandoned buildings with him. Thankfully by God's Grace, rather than accept the man's invitation, Jack ran back to the restaurant greatly disturbed by the request but never spoke of it to his parents in fear they would put a cautious end to his adventures on Main Street.

FEAR OF THE LORD

Like many cathedrals, Saint Sebastian's is one that still stands to this day on its solid foundation of masonry in the bustling downtown Middletown area. Flo's own father had been a laborer in its construction and it was modeled after a cathedral in their hometown of Milli, Italy. While the Italian Catholic upbringing was familiar to Jack because of the family's holiday visiting schedule, it was around fifth grade that he remembers their visits to Saint Sebastian's becoming a weekly part of the Sunday traditions.

As a child, Jack was in awe of the sheer wonder of the display of artistry within the cathedral. Within its hall ornate depictions of Christ and various saints filled the stained glass windows and surrounded the sanctuary with an otherworldly glow. The statues all seemed to be looking at their viewers. Jack recalls it was very intense as a child, learning the stations of the cross and rites of the church. Everything spoken and taught had a sense of authority to it, while the authority of God was understood, there were irrational fears that came from such authority. On one occasion Jack lost his rosary beads and thought God would never forgive him. Another time he had accidentally knocked a cross off the wall in a pillow fight with his cousins. Each incident created an intense sense of guilt brought on by his teachings in Sunday school. "I had started to feel that there was a God, I started talk to him every day both in prayer and in my thoughts. I knew His presence, but the religion of it filled me with fear.

Jack recalls not thinking he'd have a good little league game if he didn't pray for one, and making the sign of the cross every time he would get up to bat. The desire to have "a life for God" became a very literal interpretation for Jack. "I began to understand religion but I didn't understand faith." The rigor and exercise of the Catholic Church soon became unfitting for Jack and his family. Like him, his parents had begun to feel the rigid structures and practices of Catholicism too stringent and "a thing of man but not God." They soon found themselves at a local Full Gospel Church, where the focus was the personal study of the Bible and public worship of God.

This gathering was a more grassroots organization, though it shared a space in the Saint Sebastian's basement, it was made up of Saturday meetings and lacked the structure of the rites and practices of the Catholic church. Instead it was simply a place for people to come pray, worship and share testimony. Here, there was no hierarchy of bishops, no titles of "Father" or a designated voice of God. Here, all were welcome to speak and share of their walk with faith. At ten years old, God felt more real to Jack here, he began to read the Bible not out of instruction from his teachers but because he began to seek a relationship with God. He witnessed that those around him appeared happier and freer than those he had known in the pews of the traditional church. Though his older brother and sister, now teenagers at the time, had stopped coming to church with their parents; Jack looked forward to attending church with his parents.

He remembers seeing his Father begin to spend less time in front of the television with a beer and more time studying his Bible and his mother who had always struggled with depression seemed happier. Together they attended church every weekend, leaving the Sunday School and Catholic church behind to pursue a more personal connection with God. In one incredible moment Jack recalls a man had died of a heart attack while giving praise during a Saturday night service. "He was praising the name God in a testimony and suddenly BOOM he fell to the floor. As if God had heard his call and taken him up." Jack was impacted by the sheer faith expressed by the man. "He laid down so calm, quiet. It was clear he was not afraid of death to come. He knew where he was going."

As a young man between the ages of ten and twelve, Jack went to school, worked at the restaurant and attended services with his mother and father. "I remember, being very devout in my heart to God. I would even tell people at school that I talked to Him and they'd give me a look like I was crazy. But I didn't care." Though, like anyone, Jack was no saint. As Jack entered his adolescence he began to feel restless during his time spent in church and "Like any teenager, I got...distracted I suppose." As teenaged life began to take hold, Jack found himself talking to girls more so than God and being more concerned with using his spare Saturdays to hang out with friends rather than attend church. Instead, he'd go and hang out with his brother and the "Older Boys."

Together, Jack and Jimmy entertained the usual trials and tribulations of adolescence. Their first beers, first girls and of course first cars. Since Jimmy had a license, Jack often spent his time cruising with his brother in his 1968 Firebird. Later, Jack would get his own 1972 Duster for three hundred bucks. While it was the shell of a muscle car's former glory, together they would work on their jalopies and drive them around to see what sort of trouble they could get into. Some light pot dealing, sneaking into the drive-in theaters and some small-time arrests for teenaged disorderly conducts. Jack was living wild, wearing his "Death Before Disco" shirt, smoking, drinking and cruising around with his first love named Roanne. One adventure Jack recalls is dropping off a school friend who'd gotten too drunk only to have her parents call his house in an uproar. Luckily for him, his sister Christa was able to fake the sound of their mother's voice and let

Jack off the hook. Though it did not come without the sisterly salutation of "You owe me one punk."

During these times of adolescent freedoms, Jack recalls that it wasn't that he'd ever stopped believing in God. In fact, he'd frequently pray after some misdeed to say "I'm sorry." One of these incidents was Jack's first marijuana experience in which he felt as if he could "feel the spirit world surrounding." While the far out first toke certainly wasn't a confirmation of his beliefs, it was an indication that matters of faith still remained focal points in his perspective. For all of his wilding out with his brother and crew, Jack still remained the more innocent one. He had never been one to pick or accept fights like the other boys nor did he particularly like getting into mischief. "I was always a bit anxious, I'd be saying to myself 'oh boy, Lord please get me out of this one' though I'd get roped into some sort of shenanigans again soon enough." The older boys had picked up on it and nicknamed him "Father Jack" when they weren't praising him as "Jack Daniels."

While outside of school Jack certainly found himself in the throws of activity, so he remembers school being a much calmer place for him. He'd never had much of predisposition for any of his classes and didn't really have much thought for his future at the time. Jack spent most of his time cutting classes to hang out in the Metal Shop where his teacher Mr. Harris would let him stay as long as he had something to work on. It was during this time that Jack pursued his passion for anything with an engine, developed technical skills, and found a niche that would inspire him to later pursue a career as a technology education teacher.

One Summer Day

It was a hot day on Wednesday July 14th of 1982. School had been out for a few weeks and what time wasn't spent tending to his part time job at the grocery store, was spent as any sixteen year old's summer is; driving around with friends, sneaking off to drink and tend to the budding romance of high school girlfriends. With a day off from work midweek, it was a fitting day for teenaged spirits to take to the local beach and thrive in their summer freedom. Jack's friend Chris rang him up with the idea, then Sal, Jimmy and Charlie. Chris agreed to drive tem all in his 1970 Plymouth Duster, the same car as Jack's but in red. House by house, the boys were picked up and crammed into the two-door sportster. The thirty minute drive straight down Rt. 9 from Middletown to the shores of Hammanasset Beach was a standard portrait of carefree youth. Stolen beers, rock 'n roll and a good few miles per hour over the speed limit as the Duster cruised with its windows down, filling the car with an air of adventure. On the shores of Connecticut, shared by the Long Island Sound, Hammanesset Beach is a beach like any other. Open to the public, it's a sanctuary for the families and droves of adolescents to enjoy the heat and Atlantic waters it looks out on. The day was spent sunning, drinking and gallivanting as any would on their free day.

It was not until it came time to leave that a first sign of trouble would become premonition of what was to come. Having had enough sun and drink for the day, the boys decided to head home. "We were walking back and we noticed Chris looked a little wobbly. You could tell, ya know, that he shouldn't be driving. We asked him to give us the keys, my cousin Sal was most sober and he wanted to drive but Chris insisted. Jack recalls it was only a few moments later that Chris would back the car out too fast and catch his bumper on top of a rock. "We kept saying 'I told you. I told you.' But Chris was frustrated and told us to "hurry up and lift the car off the rock." So, they did. Jack, Sal, Jimmy and Charlie hoisted the duster free and they were off again with Chris still in the driver's seat. The Duster cruised its way back up Rt. 9 and through residential areas, dropping off Sal and Charlie at their respective homes. Charlie lived on the edge of Middletown near the more rural town of Durham. Long roads winded through its small countryside and patches of forest lined the way as the summer sun began to set. Before saying goodbye to Sal, Jack had been invited to stay the night and have dinner with his aunt and uncle. Jack declined, he had to work that evening and couldn't risk missing a shift. A reasonable excuse, Sal wished him a goodnight and told him to give him a call after work the next day. That call would not be the one expected and Jack would not make it into work that evening.

"I don't remember much really. Just a horrible noise. Sparks flying. Then, I was just...upside down. Everything hurt. Suddenly, I heard metal being ripped apart." Overturned in the forest, the red Duster laid on its back as local firefighters pried off the doors with the "jaws of life" pneumatic equipment to retrieve Jack and Chris from the wreckage. Less than a mile from Sal's house the Duster had gone down a hill and failed to navigate a sharp turn near the embankment at the bottom of the hill. The car was thrown off the road and flipped, landing on its roof and ejecting Jack through the windshield, leaving him unconscious and pinned under the upside down car with Chris in the vehicle. "I was hurting everywhere. The EMTs strapped me to a board and placed me in an ambulance. I had no idea what was happening but I was in agony." Jack was brought to the nearby Middlesex Hospital emergency room. Only a few blocks away Chris was tending to the Christian bookstore. At home cooking, Flo received the call that Jack had been in a terrible accident. In a panic, she raced to the hospital. Jack's sister, Christa came home to find unattended boiling pots, knowing in her heart something tragic had occurred. On the way to the hospital, Chris was struck by a presence. A knowing voice called out and told him Jack had a spinal injury but that he should not fear "For he will run, jump and leap for the joy of the Lord."

When they arrived, doctors lead them to Jack where they found him strapped to a board, unconscious and hooked up to life support. He was in critical condition. His spinal column had been crushed in the crash and they would need to transport him to Hartford Hospital where he would be received by the Intensive Care Unit. His fourth cervical vertebrae had broken. His fifth and sixth were cracked and there was no movement in his arms or legs. Though his left shoulder retained some movement, he was feared to be quadriplegic. "I woke up with a strange feeling that something was seriously wrong, but I didn't know what. I was face up staring at the ceiling and I couldn't move. There was this cold sensation, like a deep searing cut at the top of my head. Like an intense pressure." It was soon explained to Jack that he was in traction, a procedure intended to secure the spinal column and preserve pressure on the fractured vertebrae. A metal halo was wrapped around his head, metal screws inserted into Jack's skull to hold it in place and rigging it up to a rope with a five to eight pound sand bag. This device left Jack with chronic pain. The screws in his skull attached to the weight, felt to him as if the top of his head was going to depart at any time.

Lying in his hospital bed, attached to a weighted pulley system to keep ample pressure on his spine, Jack laid for several days in confusion as his family and doctors began to explain his condition and medical procedures. The accident, his limited mobility, his sudden pain, "Eventually, I was able to comprehend what they were saying. Essentially they were telling me I would never walk again." The news was devastating. Doctors and nurses began to speak of ways in which to prepare Jack and his family for a life of limited mobility. But something stirred in Jack. To the awe of his medical practitioners and even some of his family, Jack said "No. I'll walk again. God's going to let me walk again."

Looking back on it now, Jack still has no explanation as to why he had this confidence. The doctors and nurses wrote it off as some rebellious adolescent coping or a failure to understand the medical severities but one thing was certain, his conviction was unwavering. It was a strange hope, so sudden and fearless in the wake of such a devastating incident. "I don't know where it came from, as a teen, I always dealt with anxiety, yet, I had no fear, it can only be God. I wasn't necessarily walking the Christian life. I knew that. But something inside me just told me; "God is gonna let you walk again. He has a plan for you". And all I could do was say 'Okay Lord."

With his parents by his side in constant prayer, Jack was often reminded of the stories in which Jesus healed the sick and his conversations within became less about juvenile atonements for stolen beer or broken curfew. He no longer felt himself at a distance with his faith. For the first time he began to understand the true power of God's Word. An impeccable belief of will and trust, a knowing that everything is and will be as it should be.

Each day Jack was visited by friends and family. His room was flooded with visitors, cards from high school acquaintances and home cooked meals in lieu of whatever the hospital was passing off as edible. Over the next few weeks, Jack remained in traction and was tended to by nurses. They were kind to Jack and his family, tending to his every need. Jack recalls a nurse he nicknamed "Nurse Nightingale" after her English accent and upbeat attitude. To cheer up his cramped space in the ICU they pinned a poster of Bruce Lee and calendar to the ceiling since Jack could not turn his head. Sometimes Nightingale's boyfriend would even visit with Jack to discuss movies and monster trucks. Many were in good spirits around Jack. While they may have not agreed with his unwavering faith that he would walk again, most did not voice such opinion and were happy to see Jack retaining such optimism. Though there was one brutish nurse who filled in for the night and she told him 'Don't think I feel sorry for you.'

After a week or so, Chris, the driver that fateful night, walked into Jack's room. Much to Jack's surprise, Chris had retained little injury from the accident, a common statistic of drivers vs passengers in alcohol related accidents. Chris' visit was one of sincere apology and guilt. Standing by Jack's bed, who lay a feared quadriplegic, Chris' minorly bruised face looked down on Jack.

For many, being in such a position would inspire a sense of great injustice, betrayal and bitterness. But Jack told Chris then, just as he does now, "I don't blame him. I don't blame anyone. I never saw him as the cause. We were all guilty." Chris expressed gratitude for such grace but Jack saw guilt in his eyes. "I don't think he ever forgave himself as much as I forgave him."

As the weeks went on, no further movement was seen in Jack. His mother was struggling to believe Jack would recover, however his father had no doubt and would encourage her daily saying "If what you see when looking at Jack causes you doubt, then turn your head." The Lord had an answer for Flo's doubts, as she was praying by Jack's bed, she heard a The Holy Spirit say "Look at his hands." At this point, Jack opened his eyes and asked, "Mom, can I move my hands?" She said "Yes." At this moment Jack opened his hands for a moment, though they would not move again for 5 long weeks.

Doctors began to talk of spinal fusion surgery in an attempt to stabilize his spinal column but the expectations for full recovery still remained very low. Even if they stabilized his spine, with all the nerve damage done it would be a miracle if mobility returned. Over the week's nurses had spent every day probing with a metal pin from Jack's toe to his neck in search of nerve response but found none. Day in and day out, no change appeared to be taking place in his condition. After this surgery, there would be no further option to explore. Doctor's remained firm in their stance that Jack would spend the rest of his life in a wheelchair. But still Jack said "I will walk again. I know it."

A week after turning seventeen in his hospital bed, Jack went into surgery and a new bone was grafted into his spine via his neck. The operation was successful but uncertain if the nerve endings would be able to regenerate. "It wasn't really until then that I became a little scared. I thought after the surgery I'd be up and walking. It was very discouraging." In preparation for further rehabilitation efforts, a psychologist and social worker were assigned to Jack. Each would visit and spend time with Jack to help him prepare to face the mental and social challenges of his future life as a quadriplegic. "They'd each say 'You have to accept this.' But each time I'd just say 'No.' They were baffled. As discouraged as I was, I still believed I would walk again." Jack had a faith that was beyond his years. The medical staff was perplexed by his consistent assertions that God had a plan and that he would walk again. The social worker sent over was a younger man, who was very kind and gentle with Jack. Together they'd play checkers and try to pass the time talking about concerns of entering college, returning to his friends and how his condition would affect his social life. Jack would never fight his suggestions but always remained insistent. "I know God has a plan to let me walk again." The social worker did not object to these thoughts, yet never seemed to give them much credence. Until one day he came to Jack and mentioned how he had never been to church or prayed before but tonight, tonight he would offer his first prayer for the young man he was tending to; that brave young man who lay still in traction and immobile but somehow still believed God was going to let him walk again.

While most were receptive to Jack and his conviction, others found him trying. The psychologist, maintaining his ration skepticism of the unknowable and irrational powers of faith, at one point became very irate during a session. "If God loves you so much, why did he do this to you?" The pychologist challenged. To which Jack replied "He allowed this so you could see a miracle." It had now been a whole month that he'd spent in the cramped hospital room. Unable to move, Jack had not left his bed since his arrival. The hospital was preparing to discharge Jack and send him home with a wheelchair to begin his life as a quadriplegic. At this point the hospital staff tried to convince his family to move Jack to Gaylord Hospital, for rehabilitation for people with permanent disabilities.

Late in the night on a Friday in September, 1982 Jack was awakened by a terrible screaming. In the room next to his, a woman's screams of pain reverberated through the halls. "It sounded like hell. She was in such agony and screaming that I began to pray. I said 'Lord, lord please help her. Help her." Suddenly, Jack saw a bright green light flash before his eyes. Caught in its ethereal glow, the light suddenly shot into Jack's right shoulder and his hand sprang up! "It was like electricity. Suddenly as if someone hit my reflex, I felt my right arm and it just raised into the air on its own. And as soon as my hand raised the woman stopped screaming." The green light then vanished, as quick as it had appeared it disappeared and Jack spent the night in prayer and marvel over his sudden movement!

The following morning his family rejoiced and sang 'Hallelujah' while they watched Jack move his right arm over and over again. "Do it again. Do it again! Show your uncle," they would shout and Jack would raise his arm. When the staff returned after an extended weekend, Jack began to demonstrate some of his new function that had miraculously returned over the weekend, and the entire staff gathered around to witness his miracle. Amazed by the sudden change in his condition, the hospital decided to continue with a rehabilitation plan for Jack. He would spend the next few weeks in targeted effort to get other muscles in his arms and legs to recover mobility.

"It still wasn't any easier. Now every movement caused extreme nerve pain in the muscles. It was a sharp pain, prickling like ice to hot water. But they told me that was a good thing." Jack was the youngest person in the rehabilitation program. Due to his recent progress, he remained at Hartford Hospital Rehab instead of being transported to the Gaylord Live-In Facility. Everyone involved was enthused about the promise Jack showed with his limited arm movement but it was not without its frustration. While Jack could move his right hand, it had not returned to full strength. In one exercise he recalls being angered when a nurse would hold up his right arm and ask him to keep it there. When she removed her hand, Jack's fell straight down onto his head. "I was very discouraged. Every day they would lay me down and move my arms, my legs. The whole time I'd just say 'Okay now' only to have them fall right down."

Slowly, each day Jack's once dead body was coming to life. It was during a physical therapy session, after a few days of stagnant progress, that Jack's mom told him "Ask God to help you." Jack braced the weight and closed his eyes. "In the name of Jesus..." Jack pulled with all his might, suddenly his left arm jerked and the one pound weight lifted. It was a sign of improvement, but Jack would need to show signs of being able to walk before they could considerer discharge. Each day Jack laid in bed trying to move his muscles, with his mother and father in diligent prayer by his bedside. Rehabilitation was proving to be exhausting and discouraging. "It's the darnedest thing, you think 'Okay, I've been doing this so many days. I should be better. I should be jumping out of bed to go play baseball with my friends. Why am I just in pain?' But that was how they knew I was getting better. I remember how each time I would feel a new nerve it was like your hand had frostbite and you had set it on fire." Gradually, Jack underwent the excruciating regimen, each exercise more painful than the last. Routinely, Jack would have to be iced down to keep his muscles from tearing from the stress of parallel bars, lifts and basic calisthenics. But with each shooting pain Jack saw hope of going home.

On one such day during a session on the parallel bars, Jack made his first unassisted step. "I couldn't believe it. I was going home!" Jack began to rejoice exclaiming to doctors, nurses, friends and family "I told you! I told you! God's gonna let me walk!" Even so, his doctors remained skeptical and cautioned with every improvement "This may be as far as you get." It was only 3 weeks or so later when Jack would walk out assisted by a cane, but nevertheless walking on his own. "I remember thinking 'This is happening. This is actually happening! It's a miracle!" Together with his mother and father, a little over 2 months after first hearing he would never walk again, Jack walked out of the doors of Hartford Hospital and was brought back home.

LEARNING TO WALK

Relieved to be home and out of a hospital bed, Jack felt very much like his youthful self again. When the news got out, family and friends were quick to come to his house and witness Jack's miracle. They found him in good spirits, Jack was always thankful to have returned home and would tell anyone with ears that God had healed him. Though there was still much of His work to be done. Before Jack could be officially discharged, he had to demonstrate that he could function in a home environment. Jack had to prove that he could walk with his cane safely in his domestic surroundings. There was still concern about damage to his spinal column and Jack was fitted with a Milwaukee Brace. This was like the Halo ring used in the hospital, Jack's neck was supported by a metal bar that ran the length of his back and front torso with supports that held his chin and back of his head; a very clumsy and uncomfortable apparatus that stretched from his head to his pelvis to ensure minimum movement of the rod in his cervical spine. There was still much more rehabilitation that would be necessary before Jack could return to a full recovery. Under normal circumstances, visits to the local rehabilitation center would have been necessary but the Chamis' had the benefit and advantage in that their nextdoor neighbor was a physical therapist. Herb was a tall man with horn-rimmed glasses, a classic portrait of a medical professional, and his tone was not much different than those Jack had met in the hospital. Using an electro stimulus machine to send electrical current to muscles in Jack's arms and legs, Herb helped Jack move muscles that had been stagnant for months. Although the muscles had begun to respond, they remained in an infantile state. Jack never doubted he would recover, yet, he was not prepared for humbling experience of such clumsiness and weakness. It was a slow period of rehabilitation, but Jack was hoping to start school two months from then in November and was assuring himself that he'd be able to walk in as if nothing had ever happened.

Day by day Jack underwent his routine of therapies and a tutor was found to help him catch up with school work. His tutor was a kindly woman whom Jack referred to as "The Free Spirit", a carry over from the 60's. "I thought I had it made. With everything else considered, my days were mostly spent watching my favorite show "The Honeymooners", drinking soda and occasionally pretending not to be home when The Free Spirit showed up to do school work." Remaining true to his youthful spirits, Jack frequently talked with visiting friends about their plans for the big football games and upcoming concerts. "It's all I thought about when I got home. I was so excited to just be a kid again." While Jack retained his high spirits, there were still challenges ahead and it had not fully set in yet that his life had been changed forever.

Before Jack went into the hospital he weighed a healthy one hundred sixty pounds, but upon discharge Jack weighed one hundred and thirtyish pounds. Atrophy was a constant concern due to his inability to exercise muscles and Jack spent a good portion of his time in a wheelchair at home. Walking was possible with cane assistance but the effort was exhausting. "It was all a bit frustrating, I guess I still didn't quite get it. I didn't understand why everything was taking so long." Although Jack still held firm in his belief that it was the Lord's work and would tell anyone who listened, he was not without his disappointments.

"Your mind plays tricks on you. You wake up every day thinking things are going fast, that today BOOM your legs will pop right up. And then you go to move...and you can't" But Jack remained faithful. Though not attending church, he still believed he had been given a miracle and frequently thought back to his time in the hospital with a sense of grace and appreciation. "There were so many people I saw in there who wouldn't recover. At my appointments, I'd look around the waiting room and see so many others in wheelchairs, without legs and no chance to walk ever again. I had been given that chance." After being home for six weeks, Jack was brought back for a follow up appointment at the hospital. X-rays revealed that his spinal column had not fully recovered and in hopes of preventing further surgeries Jack would be required to wear the cumbersome bracing for an additional two weeks. Jack was stunned, he would be returning to school the following Monday. "I was very upset. I hated that thing and I knew I'd be getting a lot of attention at school. For better and worse."

For any senior, the last year of High School is a stressful last step into adulthood filled with follies of newfound freedom and overwhelming decision, never mind having to deal with a fractured spine and rehabilitation. It would be a tough and trying year. Although Jacks parents were a continual support, Jack's friends were a frequent source of levity and would transport him to and from school, pick him up for hang outs and most importantly be there when Jack once again found himself still getting into trouble. It was only during the first few hours of being back in the halls of Wilson High School that Jack was called "Frankenstein". Thank fully, a teacher heard the disruption and stepped in. Even though Jack could defend himself verbally, he had not yet realized that his mouth was tougher than his depleted body.

"Plenty of people would come up to me and say 'Hey, welcome

back!' and shake my hand. I always thought that was funny, half these people never even liked me." Though Jack recalls a most comical exchange with the head of the yearbook council who informed "We were going to dedicate the yearbook to you. But you lived, so we're honoring Bill, the janitor."

Nevertheless, Jack was happy to return to his routine. Again, he found himself returning to the solace of skipping classes and hanging out in his comfortable environment, the machine shop, where he could be with his friends and work on cars. Even Chris, the driver from that fateful night, was able to rekindle his friendship with Jack and together alongside their pals they slowly returned Jack to his teenaged norms. They snuck out of their houses to drink, mingled with girls at parties and would attend concerts. Though Jack admits there were some social difficulties with his condition, he was frail and remained dependent on a cane for mobility. "It would be embarrassing on occasion. One time at a football game I had to pee but I couldn't undo my buckle myself so I had to ask a friend to help. But they were good to me, no one ever made fun of me. Not with them." In another incident, Jack attended a J.Geils concert and was still using a cane. Amidst the crowd he noticed his cousin Linda being hassled by another concert goer. Jack made his best attempt to stop it but the harasser was underwhelmed. Until Jack's friends noticed him in a confrontation and arrived to stop the harassment. After several more weeks in the Milwaukee contraption, Jack's spinal column was finally stable and was able to support his weight, slight mobility returned to his legs and strength was building in his muscles. "I was walking. So many people couldn't believe it." In a memorable follow up appointment, Jack returned to Hartford Hospital where they congratulated him on his recovery and admitted they had no scientific explanation for such rapid recovery.

Later that day, Jack went home and triumphantly cut up the wire framed brace with a hacksaw. Excitement and joy rang throughout the house as Jack and his family celebrated another seemingly insurmountable step in his recovery. Though Jack would require a cane to walk, he had far surpassed any expectations of recovery and would only continue to grow stronger throughout the school year. However, challenges to both his rehabilitation and faith still lay in wait.

"During that time, I wasn't really thinking much. I was just excited to be back in the flow. All I wanted to do was hang out with my friends and get better so I could drive." Jack was still immature as he even broke it off with his girlfriend Tracy after she confessed 'I love you.' Without consideration for the dedication and feelings of his high school sweetheart, Jack abruptly broke off the relationship. In his adolescent mind he just wanted to catch up with all the fun. He had missed hanging with friends, being one of "the guys" and all the partying that came with it. Jack began a relationship with a cheerleader. Another, who was about to learn the disappointment of a naive heart. Jack once again dismissed a confession of love and in a tale as old as time, it was not tragedy, but a woman who disbanded Jack's friendship with Chris. Jack felt conflicted with his faith. He never doubted God's divine intervention. Along with his family he felt the Lord had touched his life, but it was still Jack's life to live. "People are funny like that. I should have sworn my life to the Lord then and there. Anything to repay the miracle I'd been given, but there I was just wanting to party with my friends again."

During the senior picnic, Jack found himself knocked to the floor after a day of drinking and losing the grip on his cane. In sheer panic he laid there unable to move or get up. "I was terrified. I thought I'd broken my neck again. Immediately I started praying 'Oh God, Oh God please let me get up.' Thankfully, I was lifted up and able to stand but I remember such an incredible fear. Never mind the embarrassment of falling in front of the whole school." The lessons of this day were not complete, as Jack would literally experience, what it means to surrender his life to the Lord later that very day.

After stealing away on a raft with friends and alcohol, Jack returned to shore and took a misstep getting out of the row boat. Again, Jack laid on the ground, fearing that he had once again broken his neck and asking himself 'What am I doing?' Jack was face to face with his reality. He was on a familiar road that he had seen so many take before him. Party to party, drink to drink, proudly living without a compass or direction. A lifetime of wandering. But Jack knew, even if he were to continue, there would still be that small voice. The one that told him, he was in need of God, and that his life was meant for more.

It was that very afternoon Jack vowed to never drink again and redevote himself to the Lord and his miracle. "There's a Bible quote that reads 'As a dog returns to his vomit, so a fool repeats his folly' (2 Peter 2:22) and it comes to mind that these were my dog days. I was putting the Lord off until I was done partying but if I had my way I'm sure that life would have ended me." Jack spent the remainder of his 17th year focusing on his academic pursuits. Jack decided to become a Technology Education teacher and would attend the local state college in the following year. He spent the summer returning to work and his car, but Jack found himself hanging out less with his party driven friends, instead was once again visiting the pews beside his parents every Sunday. "I wanted to get closer. I knew my life was His now. My life was spared by no accident and I owed Him that. I intended on finding out what a life lived totally for Him would be like, not in a formal religious way, but in a sincere heartfelt way."

Friends kept calling, old girlfriends stopped by and the tastes of alcohol remained tantalizing. Jack felt torn, he was still a restless teen who had reached a new realm of liberty in youth. But, when he was quiet and still, he always heard the words "Ask God's Spirit to govern your heart."

A NEW LIFE TAKES ROOT

On the day of his graduation from high school, Jack walked on stage with his class and received his diploma. A tremendous moment, one that only six months earlier had seemed an impossible feat. His family watched in awe at all he had overcome and the miracles that had brought Jack up those steps. Standing high up on the stage, looking upon his classmates he made an internal vow that he would live his life for the purpose God had intended when He healed him.

Jack's summer was one of solitude and devotion to his renewed sense of faith and health. Whatever time wasn't spent at his deli job at the local grocery store was spent taking long bike rides and attending church events. Though his friends would call and stop by, Jack stayed away from them to pursue spiritual reflection. He was regimented in his faith. No longer drinking, Jack would rise in the early morning for prayer and reading passages from the Bible. His inner thoughts became a prolonged conversation where Jack would hear God saying "you need the Holy Spirit in your heart." Though he invited the Holy Spirit into his heart, there were still worldly anchors pulling on his heart strings.

And so, he remained in his resolve. He remained in isolation, attended church and remained regimented in his prayer and exercise, riding his bike for mile after mile. "I knew that there was more to life than I had been asking of it." God became more real during these days. Desires felt erased and Jack felt that his heart was being changed. Toward the end of his summer, Jack recalls a moment of declaration during a prayer group session. As the hands of a church member rested over him, Jack was suddenly compelled to a word... "Surrender." Surrender, to the will of God, to His Word rather than the norms of teenage culture or society's expectations.

"I cried like I had never cried in my whole life. This feeling came over, like a sudden tension was snapped free and my struggle felt broken. I wanted to be with God more than anything in life. His peace was and is worth more than anything in this world. This was the first time I truly understood and felt that." He realized that unlike the God of his Catholic childhood, God was not a rule setter or judge presiding over his life in contemplation of heaven or hell. Jack's surrender was not one of coercion or fear, but a commitment of his heart and soul. It was no longer "I don't want to drink or etc... because I'm a Christian." It was "I don't do these things because they obstruct my relationship with God." It was this kernel of faith that would seed his relationship with much greater works to come into fruition as Jack walked again not just physically but spiritually into his new life with God's Word and

Spirit directing him.

Jack enrolled into Middlesex Community College the following fall with the help of his insurance money. He lived with his parents and commuted to school every day in an old beater car that he started up with starter fluid every morning. Intent on pursuing a career in education, Jack was struck by the degree of difficulty his course work would require. He had always managed to coast through high school but his confidence was shattered when he was placed into remedial English after an essay assignment. "I thought I had done so well on that essay. I did it on Martin Luther King and figured they'd love it but when it came back I was a bit shattered. I remember thinking I had screwed up more than I thought. I wasn't prepared." Jack stayed diligent. He remained solitary amongst his classmates and split his free time between working at his parent's restaurant and his continued involvement in the church. Here he found fellowship within his Bible study groups and a singles activity group where he would meet lifelong friends, Danny and Mike. His time of isolation had become replaced by a social group where he felt a kinship with those also devoted to their relationships with God and a passion for His Kingdom. They became his best friends and they would frequently meet not just to discuss faith but to foster a friendship on weekend trips to the movies or bike rides in their free time.

The three became a dynamic trio, brothers bonded by faith rather than blood. Jack tells of a fond story that cemented their bond with an adventure to Florida. Like any young men, they sought out a summer trip away from their families and jobs to relax on the beaches in the Florida Keys. It was a typical vacation, the trio hung around beaches, discussed their lives and what futures they saw for themselves. But one night, excitement came in through their window. Close to midnightwhile sitting on their 12th floor balcony, a horrible scream rang out. The trio looked up to discover a man was dangling from the balcony above them. A long way from the ground below. "Good lord, he must be trying to commit suicide!" one of them yelled. Immediately the three encouraged the man to come into balcony for safety. The man dropped down and the three pulled him into the room. Danny, a bit of an evangelist seeking any moment to share God with another soul, started preaching to the man. He kept telling the man, "it's not worth it, not to kill himself and that God had a plan for him." The man only became more confused, as it turned out that he wasn't trying to kill himself. He was with his ex-wife upstairs and her boyfriend had returned. He had made a drunken dash to escape. The three men faced their nocturnal intruder with a good heart, telling him they were just happy he was okay. Despite Danny's evangelism, the man quickly exited. But it was not the last they'd hear from him. Fearing that in his drunken state might be angry with them, they locked their room and made ready a closet pole for self-defense before returning to sleep. Two hours later they were awakened again this time by a knocking at their door. The man had returned, though not to commit violence. He had brought them a six pack of beer to say thanks for helping him out. "It was one of the craziest things we'd ever seen. It led to us talking about how crazy man and his desires could be. How just a few moments could end up with you dangling off a balcony near death. But I think that was the trip where we really became good lifelong friends."

TWENTY SOMETHING

Following the great Florida adventure, Jack returned to his pursuit of academics at Central Connecticut State University. This campus was larger than the community college with more vocational opportunities that even included a Christian Club for young Christians to organize. But Jack remained humble and committed to his personal place of solace. "Not much had changed for me. I didn't want to party, didn't even really want to be at school more than I had to. It was my personal accelerated program. I wanted to get my teaching degree as quickly as possible, so I applied myself completely to school when I was there. I didn't look at it as a social opportunity but a job." Despite the collegian efforts to provide students with a faith based social option, Jack recalled these groups as being very much the same as secular groups. The outworking of the group although well intentioned, did not reflect the compassion and love Jack received from the Lord. Faith was puttting out poster boards, shouted through megaphones and transcribed into organized pamphlet handouts. "That's not the way it works. People don't just get shouted at or presented with reading materials and suddenly change their minds. You have to build a relationship. They have to ask for it. It's not your responsibility to speak for God, it's your responsibility to listen for God. You demonstrate Gods love to everyone, even those who don't reflect your values."

During this time Jack retained his purposeful systems of balancing school, work and healthy relationship with his faith. His discipline remained firm and his focus on building for the new days ahead was coming to fruition. One day, Jack received a letter from his past. The return address read: Enfield State Corrections Facility. Scott. Jack had not seen Scott since sophomore year of high school. Scott had been a great friend but had always struggled with self-esteem and fallen into addiction at a young age. Scott was serving a five year sentence for armed robbery of a local gas station. When Jack had heard the news, he reached out to offer a friendship through mail. Over the years Jack and Scott exchanged letters and at one point Scott had even asked Jack to send him a Bible. Through their friendship Jack introduced Scott to a relationship with the Lord and Scott opened his heart to his faith.

This letter was an exciting one. Scott was going to be released within the month and Jack would be there to welcome him home. Scott became a fixture in Jack's life. Jack introduced Scott to his church, his friends and would spend time practicing the sacred art of golf together. Between Jack's time at school and church, Scott was often seen beside him. After graduating college in 1987,

Jack was unable to find an open teaching position and took a job painting Jack's cousin's house. He even got Scott a position working with him. Together they spent many the hours painting, and off time together playing golf or videogames. Splitting his time between the construction gig and accepting a substitute teaching job to help build his resume, Jack's time soon became sparse and he noticed Scott distancing himself. He stopped coming around after work, was less frequent to attend church events and was consistently hungover at work. "I knew and feared the worst. He had relapsed into drug use." Jack confronted Scott. Though guilty, Scott was remorseful. He needed a fresh start away from the pressures and temptation that come from living in his hometown. With the help of a local pastor, they made an overnight trip to Virginia to a Christian recovery program for addiction. It was a small ranch tucked into the Virginian mountains, a place of rest for those seeking faith based recovery.

After dropping off Scott, on the car ride back, Jack sat with his thoughts and prayed for his friend. Alcohol is one the worst addictions in the world, and by God's grace, Jack had been fortunate to escape the grasps of alcohol. But hard drugs? How could he have known how to handle this? How could he guide his friend through such peril? Deep down, Jack knew the truth. It was not up to him but up to Scott and God.

For many years, this cycle continued for Scott. Scott came out of the recovery program and stayed clean for nearly five years. After a broken ankle and prescription of oxycontin, Scott returned to a life in and out of penitentiary for subsequent possession, sales and robbery charges. "It's tragic. Really. Scott was my friend. I couldn't just watch him destroy himself. Scott didn't like what he was doing. He only felt guiltier and guiltier and that would only cause him to turn to drugs to escape. He couldn't accept the forgiveness. I never felt anger or resentment toward him. I just felt sad for him." Jack remained in contact with Scott and his family until his passing on August 20, 2020 (during which time this book was written). Spurned by his efforts with Scott, Jack later joined a prison ministry at a juvenile corrections facility similar to the one Scott had been imprisoned at. Long Lane School in Middletown, Connecticut was a corrections center that provided educational rehabilitation programs for teenage inmates. Though Jack began there as an advocate to host Bible studies, he soon heard mention of an open teaching position in the Technology Education department there. Due to his familiarity with the prison system and his resume, they were happy to offer the position to him. "To be honest they were happy to get anyone in there, the benefit for them was that they didn't have to talk me into being in a locked room with juvenile inmates." As Jack always says, "God has a plan and a purpose, opportunities are no accident."

The halls of Long Lane Penitentiary were divided onto an open campus and a confined population (a prison). Those with good behavior were afforded vocational activities like Technical Education. The student buildings were divided into two groups of eight, organized by sex and age. This area was known as The Open Campus or The Hill, just down the hill was "The Unit" aka confined population. The open air setting of the Hill campus was designed to provide a space to prepare for acclimation upon release. A chance to see a new life. It was a place of redemption for young men and women who had lost their way or never had a chance to begin with, a chance to change their lives. Jack found himself in a whole different world behind bars. While the Campus was an open air setting, there was still strict policy and procedure. Guards escorted the kids from their housing to breakfast and to their classrooms. But for the teacher, once they were in your classroom they were under your care. "It wasn't like you couldn't call for help if you needed it, but you were responsible for any incident related to or within your classroom. Which, I don't know if some of the higher ups had ever had to handle before. I mean, I had to count the screwdrivers every day in fear of someone stealing one and using it for violence. At times I became paranoid." The politics of a prison culture were often found to be inconsistent and difficult to navigate. "Some staff were too strict, I think in some way on a power trip and they would be absolutely cruel to the inmates. But others were too idyllic and couldn't understand why a group therapy session couldn't stop a fight. It was a tough balance."Jack tried to focus his best on those who could benefit from his classes. There were many different types of offenders in his classroom, however the real troublemakers tended to weed themselves out quickly. There was always some reason to be concerned. One time returning from his lunch break, Jack pulled into the prison parking lot to find two girls running across the lot. A prison break! Spurned by his fight or flight instinct, Jack immediately shifted his car into reverse in attempt to cutoff the escape. Jack found himself racing down the street in reverse in an overzealous attempt to prevent an escape. However, they dodged him and Jack sat halted wondering "What am I doing?" It wasn't his job to be a security guard and sure enough security caught up with the escapees. Eventually after being caught and serving time in the "Unit", Jack saw them in his class. They laughed and told him "We were thinking about jumping you and taking your ride but decided not to." In good humor Jack laughed off the chance encounter, but became a bit more wary of his surroundings and students. "Although, I was hired as a technology education teacher, my job was more that of a counselor. It broke my heart to see kids that for many reasons, never truly had a fair chance to succeed in this society."

From the age of twenty three to thirty, Jack would work here teaching technical skills to those ready for release. While there was always some form of excitement happening, Jack felt he did good work there and much of his time was spent fostering an education in those who had not had the chance before. By taking one step of faith by volunteering to lead a Bible study for incarcerated teens, Jack had been guided to a seven year journey in Corrections where he felt his work he accomplished more than earn a paycheck.

DESIRE OF MY HEART

At the age of twenty seven Jack felt he had found his rhythm in life. What time he spent outside the halls of penitentiary he spent with his family and his church. An investment by his father many years ago had brought his family further into their faith and Jack's intimate circles became one and the same. A sense of balance had been achieved. His friends, his family and his recreation were all united by faith. But as with any man's quest or venture in this life, he found something was still missing. There was a gnawing, a call to serve more directly in the name of God.

After a friend of the family returned from Bible college, Jack's family found themselves at a small church housed in a modest grange hall, a tradition of farmers handed down as a space for community gatherings. In this space, the church held firm to its grass root stable. There were not pews but foldable chairs. No incense or wafers nor any real sense of religious iconography. Only small Bibles in the hands of an at capacity room of fifty or sixty people. The pulpit was not off limits, but shared by those in the congregation who wished to testify of their success and tribulations with faith.

Aside from worship and testimony, the church provided a social haven for its members. Jack's time spent away from work would most likely find him out on a golf course, those sharing in the despair of the back nine of fellow Christians. The church held its services on Sundays and on Saturdays, and held organized social outings. A group dubbed "Singles Club" provided a sense of camaraderie for Jack within the church. "Making friends is not easy. Dating's even harder! But combining those with faith? It can be the trickiest of all." The group would accompany each other and provide opportune first dates with outings to movies, batting cages, golf courses and dining.

It had been eight years since his accident and separation from his high school sweetheart. Jack had not been pursuing any romantic relationships. Throughout the years Jack had devoted his energies to becoming right with himself and his faith. Putting trust in his faith, Jack felt that in time God would provide everything and everyone he needed. But it had been a long time. "I was feeling somewhat frustrated. Working at the prison was wearing on me, I was hoping to find a public school position. I still lived with my parents and still hadn't truly found anyone I was attracted to." Jack was holding strong to the promise he had felt God made to him once. In a vision, God had shown him the solar system and said "Until I become the center of your universe, I will not add another." Since that moment Jack had remain dedicated in his trust and relationship, but he hoped still it would be six to twelve months not ten years of waiting for his bride.

One afternoon on a warm summer day in August 1991, a lifelong family friend named Dolores came running into the house. Finding Flo in the kitchen, she exclaimed "She's here! She's here! Jack's Angel!" Intrigued as any mother would be, Flo stood and listened as Dolores told her about "the most beautiful girl who came to church today."

Megan Wheeler was a young red haired daughter of an Irish father, Neil Wheeler, and Nordic mother, Sandra "Sandie" Heike. Though small in stature, her smile and laugh could fill a room. She had not grown up in Connecticut or even on the east coast. Coming to the east coast after graduating from the University of Washington, Megan had accepted one of the only residencies available for pediatric orthotics and prosthetics. Having to choose between Minnesota and Connecticut to pursue her degree in spinal bracing it was decided that she would head for the opposite coast. "It's a funny thing, I remember hearing about Connecticut as a child and just knowing I'd end up there some day." To this day, she still cannot recall what exactly it was that put it in her heart.

"My God! isn't that ironic?" Flo exclaimed. Jack was just on a vacation trip to see a church friend whose family lived in Seattle. After returning few days later Jack was told by his mother and Dolores of their shared prophetic gossip. "She's the one" Flo declared.

The following Sunday Jack paid very close attention to the new comer. He strategically procured a seat in the row behind her. Her strawberry hair hung with a glow and her voice sang out with perfect melody. Her skin seemed to glisten as she raised her hands in praise. Suddenly, Jack's heart seemed to stop beating, his eyes became fixated on her left hand. A small diamond ring.

Though, honoring the commitment of the ring was his intention, Jack felt great disappointment. "Thou shalt not covet thy neighbor's wife". The words of a most High command echoed in his brain. But following the service he found himself approached by Megan. She had heard he was in Seattle and wanted to introduce herself. Conflicted by his guilt and stunned by her beauty Jack managed to tell her of his time there and asked if she was making friends. Citing the struggle of any newcomer, Megan confessed she wasn't, though she shared a room with two other interns. Summoning his best face as a friend, Jack invited her to the following weeks Single Group outing.

The outing took place at the pier in Old Saybrook and the group decided to go crabbing. One would tie a piece of chicken on a string and toss it into the waters to fish for the occasional blue crab that would come ashore. Though she was the daughter of an ocean loving fisherman, Megan allowed Jack to show her the peculiar tactics. After proudly demonstrating how to tie a piece of chicken to a string and when to pull, he asked; "Are you…are you engaged?"

When asked about the ring, Megan went flush with embarrassment. It was not an engagement ring. It was a promise ring. Back in Snohomish, her home town in Washington, Megan had been dating Mark, the friend of her sister's boyfriend. Mark was a roofer and had been Megan's boyfriend for a year now. He'd given her the promise ring before she took her trip out. As any long distance relationship goes, the phone lines kept them connected every few nights a week following her shifts at Newington Children's Hospital.

Having asked about her ring, Megan inquired about Jack's limp in his right leg. Sitting on the dock with his legs dangling over the water and their shared fishing string Jack told Megan the tale. His tales of teenaged drinking, the accident, his commitment to the Lord, his recovery. And then the relapse and dwelling of faith he'd committed to the years. "How could you turn back after such a miracle?" Megan remarked. A shock went through Jack's system.

But something about the way she smiled at him when she said it put an ease to his sense of rejection. Quoting Popeye Jack's only response was "Ay'am what ay'am". That afternoon was further spent pursuing the blue crab and swapping stories of their upbringing. "I became close with him very quickly. Just as a friend but there was something about him. I immediately knew who he was. Down to earth, kind and not afraid to just be himself." Megan recalled.

Megan kept a lively friendship with Jack through the following months. They spent their time among the Singles Group and became intimate friends. One movie night the two found themselves outside only to talk for several hours. Jack wasn't a fan of Silence of the Lambs, psychological movies always got stuck in his head. Megan didn't like the blood. Instead they talked about their upbringing and faith. Megan was raised Lutheran but similar to Jack had left the faith as a teenager only to rededicate herself in her college years. Like Jack she appreciated the simplicity of a small church atmosphere and its focus on faith over religious rigor.

"I was absolutely taken by her. I mean we were total opposites. I grew up in an Italian Catholic family without many life goals. She was reared in a reserved traditional American family. But at the same time, she felt like a kindred spirit." Jack's intentions began to compound against his respect to her out of state courtship. On a visit to a local fair Jack would count the line to the Ferris wheel and coordinate his position in the cue for any chance to sit next to Megan. In another effort, he spent fifty dollars on a carnival game to win her a $5 teddy bear.

A few weeks before Thanksgiving Megan received word that Mark wanted to come out and visit. The relationship had become entangled in the phone lines and Mark felt it would help if they saw each other to iron it out. Megan confessed she felt the relationship was waning and agreed. The following Saturday Jack was mortified to see Megan standing with Mark in Jack's parents' living room for movie night. Polite, Jack shook his hand, but from the back of the room all night he watched their hands. His around hers, a tight grip that didn't want to let go.

Jack stayed away from Megan and his thoughts of her during the duration of Mark's stay. On the following Sunday Jack saw Megan again in church but noticed something was different. There was no ring on her finger. Jack nearly leapt out of his skin before he asked what had happened. Megan confessed that although Mark was kind, her heart was speaking differently. She didn't have the proper words for it but she was confident that promise ring had to return to Seattle. She was hearing a new direction from God for her life. "I nearly exploded. This was too hard to believe." Jack immediately began to hatch his proposal to take Megan out on a formal date. However, within two weeks Megan received word that her grandmother had passed away, so she would be spending her holidays back in Snohomish to be with her family. Jack offered his condolences but also held a secret fear. During her time at home Megan would see Mark again. With such tragedy in her

family Jack feared she might never return to Connecticut and might decide to finish out her degree closer to home.

With a heavy heart, Jack underwent his holidays. For many weeks he thought about calling her, but felt he would overplay his hand and his guilt would fester. He prayed about his feelings, asserted his faith in God's plan. Despite any romantic connection, Jack's heart felt empty until one day he received a Christmas card in the mail. It was from Megan and one of the fonts had a smiley face drawn in it. "I felt like a little boy on Valentines, I was so excited to receive a card from Megan Wheeler." Shortly after Christmas, Megan reappeared at a Sunday service. She shuffled her way next to Jack and he turned to ask her a life changing question. "Do you like hockey?" The two had their first date at The Skywalk Restaurant that over- looked Main Street in Hartford where they sat to eat before grabbing their tickets for a local Hartford Whalers game. As they sat, each confessed their hearts to one another. "I had no idea!" Megan exclaimed when Jack confessed to his fairground antics. "Since the day I met you" he said. Following the hockey game, the two continued to talk late into the night and even decided to make a phone call to her parents. Though not a formal proposal, both Jack and Megan knew they wanted to spend the rest of their lives together. The next day, they made a phone call to the west coast. "I knew it. I knew! You were always mentioning him!" said Megan's mom, Sandie, when Megan informed she was now with Jack. From that night forward the two entered more of an engagement than a casual dating experience. The two became inseparable and six months later on June 27, 1992 they were married. "We both knew God would guide us. We trusted Him individually and He ended up bringing us together. That was what we believed. There was no chase, everything unfolded to the plan of God."

A NEW ERA

With the love of his life consecrated in marriage, Jack moved out of his parent's home and rented an apartment. Though they would not be here long, it would prove the first home for Jack and Megan to call their own. The start of a not just a new life but a family. Continuing in their career pursuits, Megan finished her internship and Jack was beginning to plan his exit strategy from the prison halls into public schools. Life was beginning anew for the young couple and with the discovery of Megan's pregnancy a few months following their marriage, it would only continue to bloom.

However, just as the virtues of their love flourished under the rays of their faith, in others they saw it began to wilt. What had been a familiar place of rest and spirit began to look strange to them with the arrival of a new minister at the church. In the small grange hall, the young couple began to sit week after week and noticed the pews being vacated by friends following every sermon. The words on the pulpit seemed to become less about earnest spirituality and more focused on spectacle tactics. Members of the church were called up to the front of the room and chastised under the guise of spiritual insight.

"Leadership is supposed to be an anointing of God. When it's real it speaks to other hearts, it doesn't just fill the heart of the leader. With his new direction it was 'God knows you are doing this and you must do this!' In Jack's eyes he saw not a minister but a showman. Seeing this new approach as ministry through judgment, it recalled his days of the fear mongering priests and their sense of grandeur over their parishioners within his Catholic childhood. This minister did not last very long but much of the damage had been done as the parish splintered before his departure. The new minister did not reflect the heart or spirit of the founding pastor and his wife, the heart that had drawn Jack and Megan to this little church. Just as they were beginning a new life together, Jack and Megan would embark on a new spiritual journey.

At the recommendation of one of the fleeing flock, Jack and Megan found another church in Southington, that was preaching a familiar message. On the steps of a Church with four large pillars stood erect and held a vast roof over its immense house of worship. This was no grange hall, no basement but certainly no cathedral either. The size of the building was certainly impressive but within its walls Jack and Megan felt a familiar warmth.

Much of the congregation was made up of young families and couples, some familiar faces had already transplanted from the former church to welcome them and the always exuberant words of the Pastor echoed a simple truth that Jack and Megan had come to embrace. Raised in a Italian immigrant family, the Pastor felt familiar to Jack and his messages carried a certain excitement that came not from the stage of the pulpit but from above it. He was laid back, contemporary and spoke of the relationship, love and compassion that faith requires. The church provided many outreaches which focused on family and youth programs. There was even a leadership program in place for those who sought to do more within the church's infrastructure. With a child on the way and a vision for their new life together, Jack and Megan saw the perfect garden in which to plant their first seeds together.

Now at about 7 months pregnant, Megan was preparing to take her orthotics board exam and she remained at Newington Children's hospital to complete her residency in preparation for the exam. Jack continued to teach at Long Lane School and also became involved in the church. He volunteered, fostered new relationships and became a familiar face at the church rather quickly. What time was not spent at work was spent at the church or tending to the care of his wife as they awaited the birth of their son. Jonathan Michael Chamis was born April 14th 1993 in a Middletown hospital, a short distance away from their small apartment. As any parent will say, life soon became a complex juggling act. Jack was a full time teacher, an evening student pursuing his Master's in education, a church volunteer, but most importantly a husband and a father. Megan was home to raise her son but she was never one to keep still for long. Together the two found themselves volunteering to head up the youth group at church and they began taking smaller leadership roles within the church.

A few months after their son's birth they decided to move into a new home, a little house tucked into a wooded lot in rural Durham. It was just a few miles from Middletown and only a couple hundred yards down the road from where Jack had that fateful car accident. "It was a bit surreal. I would drive by that spot every day going to and from that house. And every day I had a reminder of what had happened...then I would come home, open the door and just feel it. Everything that could've been taken away by that moment but also everything I had I also had because of it." It had only been by a sheer coincidence and affordable price that put Jack and Megan in that house but such coincidence is often that which inspires a certain sense of divine intervention. During the first year Megan had the privilege of caring for Jonathan before returning to work as an Orthotist. However, Megan was only back to work eight weeks before finding out that she was again pregnant. Hannah Elizabeth Chamis was born January 13th 1995. With both a daughter and son to take care of, Jack and Megan's lives became increasingly consumed with family, work and spending what time they could with the church.

It was during this season of increased responsibility and economic pressure that Jack started to struggle with anxiety. Jack began to have obsessive fears. Though no longer working for the prison system he would recount screw drivers and tools over and over in his head. The former routine became an obsessive thought. While he never went for professional help, he began to read various books to find solace in his faith. One particular title called "The Battlefield of the Mind" struck as a revelation for Jack. The Christian tradition instilled in Jack growing up was not "Faith in God" but "Fear of God". A fear which still lingered within and was inducing Jack's anxieties. Through Jack's study and pursuit to further his relationship with God, Jack found insight into the love and forgiveness that would inspire his pursuits and quell his fears into faith.

Megan returned to work part-time at the Children's Hospital which had moved from Newington to Hartford and Jack was able to find an opening in the Hartford public school district. Together the two found both a balance and struggle in building their new life. New goals, new jobs, new responsibilities and at the same time finding time to nurture their faith.

The church's "Leadership In Ministry" program was designed as a certificate program for those looking to step into a leadership role. While Jack had found that being a Youth Group leader was not his forte, he was keenly aware that each day that he awoke and he could stand to his feet was a day to walk in the purpose that God had ordained. There was a burden not of debt, but a goal to let no opportunity go to waste. Jack had remained very involved with volunteering his time at the church and developed many relationships. When he heard about this new opportunity he felt it in his heart to enroll. "I thought I was crazy. Everything was full time. Full time teaching, full time schooling (it would be another two years of night classes before I got my Master's degree), full time father...but I had to do it. I always knew I had to do it. Yet, I was always looking for open doors to God's purpose." Jack completed both degrees in 1997 and was accepted as a member of the church's leadership team. With the children coming to school age, Megan was able to work four days a week and found herself fulfilling a leadership position of her own.

As one of the few women in a male dominated workforce at the time, she became a guiding figure for other women stepping into the field of Orthotics. "To serve God doesn't have to necessarily take place within church walls or Biblical text. Just helping others along their life journey is God's will. That was where I excelled. It's so important to find a purpose in your occupation. Be fulfilled, connect with patients and residents. But it's also important to be able to come home."

Megan often extended herself to other working mothers in the field, offering guidance and encouragement as they too found a balance in their own lives. "In many ways the time away from the office was hardest part for me. I had just been accepted when I got pregnant and knew I couldn't just wait around. I would grow anxious. Being able to work part time really made me a better mother but it's not easy and it's not the same for everyone." Megan was young in her career and was faced with the well understood challenge of balancing the aspirations of work and home. She was privileged to work part time as a young mom but kept engaged with her career.

As the years went on, the young family found themselves settling into Southington. It was closer to Megan's work and the church was only a few minutes away. With the expected arrival of another daughter, Madelyn Rose Chamis, on December 17th 1999 and a house in the vicinity of three public schools, 68 Dawn Lane became the home front for the next 18 years of their lives. The house stood as one of many along the road to a cul-de sac. Sidewalks winded through the neighborhoods to a charming downtown shopping center and winds whisked the cheers of children playing across the lawns.

Their children grew through the years often thinking of the church as a second home. Jack had become an established figure in the leadership there and Megan was again finding herself the head of the children's group at church. What time wasn't spent in school or running through the neighborhood was spent amongst other families and their children at church. In many ways they had found their balance.

But school years began to weigh on Jack. He was a very involved teacher. He often volunteered for after school programs and was awarded "Teacher of the Year" in 2004. He had become a department head a few short years after his tenure there and found himself in a very secure position. He was afforded summers off which gave time for trips to visit Megan's family and gave him time with his children. All along with a decent salary that kept things financially stable.

When an assistant pastor position became available, Jack once again felt the nudge of God's spirit. Another door was opening. It would be a huge step of faith. Both Megan and Jack knew he would be accepted. But the pay would barely scratch what he made as a teacher and offered no benefits, just as Megan was about to return to a full-time position.

"It was very stressful. I questioned myself a lot during that year. What would people think? Would my children starve? What if I fail?" But each day Jack sat at his desk in his classroom, the more he knew he didn't want to do this for another fifty years. "My heart and mind kept going back to the 'Green Light.' I know the Lord had divinely healed me for a purpose."

The discussion went on for several months. Megan was very pragmatic and analytical. Her family had raised her with a strict sense of work ethic and security. The thought of Jack leaving that behind challenged her. Over the years she had heard of Jack's desire and knew his heart was in it. But raising a family, just about to reach a full-time position as a working mother…" I knew it wouldn't add up. Bibles don't turn a profit. Not the right ones anyways." Her heart however remained open as Jack explained himself.

Jack often thought back to his own parents in those moments. They had lost everything, their homes, their families and their businesses. They were never rich but they always had each other. Against the grain of American materialism, they had always spoken of a most cherished possession "Faith." Sitting in his office chair Jack thought back to the times he sat in his wheelchair and those first steps he took. "I was already physically paralyzed, I did not want fear of failure to spiritually or emotionally paralyze me."

With Megan's blessing Jack turned in his final notice at work and accepted the position of Assistant Pastor at the church. "When I told my co-workers where I would be working, people didn't know how to respond. When I would walk through the halls of the school and tell people why I was leaving they would give me strange looks. No one understood. To that I just had to smile. I knew." Jack began his tenure as an assistant pastor and would spend the next five years serving the church and his faith full time.

PASTOR JACK

Jack's new life in full tenure as an assistant pastor came as a whirlwind. Being one of the two pastors at the church Jack found his life transformed by his new duties. Weddings, funerals, counseling, outreach programs and facility managment. There was no longer a Monday to Friday, nine to five schedules. Any day at any time Jack made himself available to tend to the congregation and pursue his passion. "My first year felt very much like a trial by fire."

Much of Jack's work was mostly managing the projects within the church. He would organize volunteers in outreach programs, assign leaders for children's church and head up several programs in his best attempt to keep the church vibrant. While at times stressful, this was very much regarded as the lighter work Jack occupied himself with. As an assistant pastor, one of the many duties is to provide counseling. In a sacred privacy Jack would meet with those both from within the church or referred to him from the community. In these sessions Jack would often be faced with difficult challenges. Still a young man he often found himself counseling older couples. It was an eye-opening experience for him. "You wouldn't believe it sometimes. People could completely disrespect each other, cussing and all. Right in front of me. Then

Sunday I would see them and they would appear 'normal.'" Jack was learning the curious nature of faith and human nature. Again, God was making it very clear to Jack how the two kingdoms collide until a person decides to yield their hearts to God's ways.

In one counseling session within his first year Jack met with a young woman. She was a single mother of two and was again pregnant. She was struggling emotionally and was being tempted to consider an abortion. "I remember being so scared this was bigger than anything I'd faced before. This was a child's life. Did I say the right thing? Could I have said more? What if she does it? What if it's my fault?" In the end Jack knew to hold to his resolve. The child's life was not in his hands but the Lord's. A few years later Jack was informed that the child had been born and the woman was a happy mother.

Jack was sometimes called on to attend those in the hospital. There was one instance where Jack stood over a man in a coma from a suicide attempt. Jack did not know the man but his family had called and asked him to pray. "In so many of those situations I had to have the utmost trust in the Lord. I would literally pray in my head saying 'Lord I don't know how to bring light into this darkness. Give me the words."

There was once a man who lost his wife suddenly, and a year later on the anniversary of his wife's death, he lost his daughter to overdose of heroine. Jack officiated both of these funerals. "90% of people are trying their hardest. If you don't believe that you're going to be frustrated, nobody wants to be miserable."

While Jack loved meeting new people it was on Sunday mornings that he felt most fulfilled. Every six weeks and Jack was allotted a Sunday sermon to provide relief for the Pastor. It was here that Jack felt truly at peace. No longer teaching technical matters to teenagers with no interest, Jack discussed topics of spirituality focused on relationship and humility. The church was very responsive to Jack's humble tone. His words came not from a study of theology but a brokenness that reflected our own human flaws and failures. He spoke not of what God wants of us to be but us wanting for God. A life lived not within words but action.

For the most part Jack felt the shared spirit of the church, yet once again Jack's heart felt restless. He was getting that "nudge" again. The same nudge that had called him to step out in faith and leave the security of a twenty-year teaching career. Was there something else to pursue? Was God the author of this restlessness and causing Jack to search his heart for something new...again?

The vision of the church was expansive. Jack remained humble and sought to fulfill his duties but the distinguished difference in leadership styles was becoming apparent. Although Jack had become comfortable and established, there was talk of handing the church over to Jack in the future. While this was a generous offer, Jack became more and more disturbed by the thought of settling. And again, he felt the nudge. About five years into his tenure, during a men's retreat during the summer, Jack heard the Lord speak vividly for one of the few times in his life. Almost 25 years ago the Lord had told him he would walk when he was paralyzed. Now out under the summer night sky and following a worship service Jack heard Him call again. There's a story in the Bible about Jacob, Abraham's grandson. He wrestled with God as he was a con artist type of character. God wanted him to be his servant and Jacob would try everything to outwit and wrestle with God. To humble him the Lord touched him in hollow of his side and Jacob limped the remaining days of his life. Eventually, the Lord changed his name Jacob ("Conniver") to Israel ("Prince of God") From Jacob, God birthed the nation of Israel. Jack had always related his spiritual journey to the story of Jacob. But on this night Jack heard a voice inside him say "Stop relating to yourself as Jacob (conniver, unprocessed by God) and begin to see yourself as Israel (servant of God, processed by God). The preparation is complete. You are ready for my service."

It was in this moment that Jack was struck with the courage to step out in faith and start a church. Once again, God was asking him to walk on water. From leaving the security and provision of a 20 year teaching career to now stepping out of the boat of security of an established church and plant an independent seed in the soil of Rocky Hill, CT. In a town where he had once taught middle age students the wisdom and genius of Edison he would now bring the life altering Gospel of Jesus Christ. The Lord had prepared Jack well under the spiritual leadership of his pastor and the life lessons of a 20 year teaching career.

While contemplating what God was requiring of him, Jack would hold off on his resignation for the time being he began to explore the courage and faith within himself. It was during this time that a friend gave him a book entitled "You Can't Walk On Water Unless You Get Out of The Boat". This became a mantra for Jack. During this time, Jack upheld his duties at the church but began to feel awkward. "Suddenly, I felt inspired, I knew I was equipped and ready to step into what God had prepared me to do over a lifetime of lessons. Nothing was wrong, I just had to take that step of faith and walk on the path God's spirit was requiring of me." At long last it became time for Jack to announce his resignation. The lead pastor felt caught off guard and as he assumed Jack had been on board with future plans for the church. Perhaps Jack hadn't sent enough signals, or perhaps when one is focused on their own vision, he doesn't see another's. Though he had not secured a location yet, the chairs around the living room began to grow and Jack's ministry was taking formative steps. A small group of close friends and family was assembled to become the first members of his new mission. In the living room of one of their houses they would meet to discuss faith and future plans.

"If it wasn't for God speaking to me again I would've thought I was crazy. The first step into pastoring had already been scary and here I was just a few years later saying I was going to start my own church." Being a minister had never been prosperous and what money he had would only sustain his family for months, not years.

Jack desired to establish a grass roots family oriented ministry. While this wouldn't require a grandiose church, he needed to find a location to dig his foundation. There were many struggles associated with planting a church at this time. Many landlords often find religious establishments less than desirable due to their lack of retail value. To compound the matter, the United States was still rebounding from the 2008 recession. Most facilities were falling out and shopping plazas were being deserted by bankruptcy. Jack also worried about starting off on the wrong foot by settling too close to the previous church. While it was desirable to be close to home in Southington, there was already a subtle tension over former members who had joined Jack's ministry. Rocky Hill had always been in Jack's heart. He had always felt God leading him there. This was the former school district where he had taught middle school, it was a similar area to Southington and only a twenty minute ride up the interstate. Jack inquired with many desperate landlords but was met with much rejection. He would make calls only get hung up on as soon as the word 'church' was uttered, yet he continued to hunt through any listings for available space.

One afternoon, in desperation, Jack wandered into a large technical trade school in Rocky Hill. There was no listing for a room to rent but Jack liked the location as it was close to the highway and decided to inquire. The receptionist seemed taken aback by the suggestion that a technical school would rent out their rooms to a church but Jack politely asked to speak with a manager. The manager met Jack with quite the contrary response. The idea of a church renting a room thrilled him. The founder and owner of the institute was a Christian himself and Jack could not only rent the room but the whole building for only five hundred dollars a month.

A fire lit under Jack that day. Immediately he made plans to utilize the gift but found he needed something. A name. It was from that moment on that the ministry The Oasis of Life was established. A name Jack had suggested years earlier for a prayer room at his previous church that had been dismissed. Yet, when packing boxes to move out of his former office, he came across the sign he had made for it and could not bring himself to throw it away. Fliers, cards and signs were created and spread amongst the community. Jack's leadership team consisted of those from the initial living room group, all who had worked to help promote the new ministry.

Sure enough, every Sunday morning from 8am to 11am the Porter and Chester Institute in Rocky Hill, CT was transformed into The Oasis of Life Christian Church. An audio/visual system was wheeled into the small classroom to provide worship and the ability to hear the message of this new ministry. It lacked any semblance of a formal church and was certainly a far fetch from any cathedral. For every ten people who showed up, perhaps one would stay and become a part of the Oasis community. A small family began to form and Jack felt his mission was taking root. The mission statement for the Oasis of Life Christian Church became "A place of refuge and refreshing" was coming to fruition. Jack's leading principle was to give every member a voice. He led Oasis with this verse from Ephesians in mind; "Every joint supplies the body."

Churches often replicate the society they live in rather than transform it. They tend to elevate figureheads rather than utilize the individuals with gifts from the local church body.

Jack made every attempt to go against the grain of the star

driven society in which we live. Periodically, members were given opportunity for open forum, though at times Jack admits it became a bit chaotic. Infrequently, someone would interrupt his sermon for their own purpose and he would have to find some balance of control. But for all intents and purposes the Oasis of Life was a collective; a true church family.

Once the essential elements of the church were in place, Jack knew it was time to find a job, as the church at this time could not afford to support his salary for his family. Money began to get tight and he needed to find another job. "I went against a life principle that the Lord had crafted in my life; 'Wait on the Lord.' But I panicked and went back to teaching school. I knew in my heart, I was deciding to return to teaching from a place of fear. I struggled a lot with my return to teaching. I was able to secure a teaching position, but not in the familiar surroundings of a small town like Rocky Hill, but an inner city school in Waterbury. But I needed some more income. Not just for me but for my family."

After a few months balancing his church duties with teaching, Jack asked God to forgive him for making this terrible mistake. He asked for a way out of the position secured in fear. It was the next day that his cousin Glenn offered him a job with his development company. Jack was able to leave his teaching position and take the job at his cousin Glen's development firm. "I was definitely a fish out of water in comparison to teaching. I was never good at sitting at a desk, looking at graphs etc. But it paid enough to pay the bills and gave me some insights into management and organizational skills." Once again, Jack knew in his heart, the Holy Spirit was teaching him another life lesson, if he was willing to be teachable.

Once the essentials of the church were in place, Jack knew it was time to find a more permanent location for the church. The nation was still recovering from the financial crisis of 2011 when Jack found a new location for The Oasis of Life. A storefront in the Cold Spring Plaza just off the main road near I-91 in Rocky Hill. It is here that the Oasis of Life still stands to this day.

THE OASIS

The new location for The Oasis of Life Church in Cold Spring Plaza, like many shopping centers, had seen many different occupants throughout the years; restaurants, nail salons, big businesses, small businesses. But never had it held a church until the Oasis of Life banner hung from one of its doorways. Through renovation what had formerly been an Italian restaurant that could have doubled for a scene from The Godfather became a center for worship. The old kitchen in the back was converted into classrooms and the bar still remained but now served complimentary coffee. Through its doors one walked in only to find Jack's office taking the place of a hostess booth. The total renovation took over three to four years to complete and included not just the development of the building but the growth the congregation from a handful of members to numbers nearing a hundred.

"It was always both nervous and exciting. I'd see a new family come into church and think 'Wow, five more people than last week!' only to then see four fewer the next week. I'd drive myself crazy sometimes wondering if I said something wrong or needed to do something different." The growing pains felt hardest in the first five years, for many a mile mark of success or failure. Throughout the years Jack had seen many start to plant their own churches only to pack it up due to various reasons.

Jack recalls meeting a minister who had just moved from North Carolina. He was planning on starting up a church and asked Jack for some advice. Jack offered his heartfelt thoughts, from a lifetime of growing up in former immigrant communities that remain as Catholic strong holds in terms of faith. "I could tell by his responses, he felt like I was a bucket of cold water on his passionate dreams. Yet, in my sincerity, I was simply trying to prepare him for the battle ahead."

New England holds a precarious mixture of faith. While settled by Protestants fleeing the Church of England, they themselves formed their own rigid establishments that burrowed into the grounds of the region and remain steadfast to this day. There are many sects and denominations of Catholics, Protestants, Baptists etc. New England is home to the majority of Catholic churches within the U.S largely due to its influx of European migrants. The churches are old, familiar and long established. New church missions like the Oasis of Life Church occupy a classification of 'non-denominational' for lack of better descriptors. Unable or unwilling to define themselves by edict or denomination, they remain committed to the gospel as the road map to guide the Christian on his or her individual journey. This is the school of thought for those in the grassroots movement of contemporary Christianity. Jack has observed; "Most faith based establishments, even some 'non-denominational' missions, are based on figureheads. Since the times of Rome, the whole business model of faith has been a system that elevates men as priest or a minister. Anything that does not have Christ at the center will end in corruption. As soon as the church emulates the society your in, you are in trouble."

Jack was taxed by all the natural anxieties that come with an independent venture. Guided by his strong sense of faith he felt he could only do what felt authentic to his faith. He kept his mission focused on evolving away from the old church model and developed a model he calls 'relational leadership.' Using a collective framework Jack organized a small group of leaders to not only assist in church operations but to have a say in the direction of the church. No decision could be made by one single person, not even Jack himself. The team was made up of volunteers, Jack and his leaders worked to facilitate various community outreaches and operations of the church. "It's never difficult to find people who need help. That's always the easy part, all you have to do is have a good spirit and a willing heart. But I'll admit at times I can be a bit too laissez-faire. I'm not much of an organizer. I tend to just get up and do. So, I rely on other people just as much as anything. I always have to remind myself 'Don't try to do too many things. Better one thing done well, then five half done."

One program developed by the Oasis team was the mission to help the local community with food needs, which led to a partnership with the non-profit Foodshare program. In effort to combat hunger for those in need, Foodshare works with any organization seeking to bring hunger relief to their area. Small businesses, charities, churches only have to meet the criteria of having a minimum of ten volunteers and a designated space to engage the community. When Jack proposed bringing the food program to Rocky Hill he was met with a surprising amount of resistance from locals. Being an upper middle class town, some felt confused and concerned about gathering homeless or low-income citizens in their local park every other Friday. Per regulation Jack was required to seek town permission, and he did receive it.

Elm Ridge Park is a small city park comprised of a parking lot next to a couple of baseball fields and a pool. It is mostly empty during the week while children are at school and the only occasional disturbance is a duck stopping its flight to take a break on the swings. Yet every other Friday, one hundred or more people gather in the parking lot and line up to receive food from a Foodshare truck and the Oasis ministry team. "The most important thing is to smile," Jack frequently told volunteers. Nearly 60% of those in the food line are elders who have exhausted their benefits or resources. The other 40% are families. They come from small towns within a twenty-minute drive, upper middle class communities, similar to Rocky Hill, where upon first glance one wouldn't even think there would be homeless amongst the countless cul-de-sacs.

During these events Jack does all he can to make it cheerful. He frequently encourages volunteers to talk to the people not about spirituality but life. "Tell them a joke. Ask about the weather. Etc etc. If someone wants to hear about your faith, they'll ask you. But that's not what we're here for. We're here to meet their needs and to help." To further the Spirit of blessing, a free raffle is held prior to the food distribution, the winner receives a gift card to the local supermarket. Within the walls of the Oasis of Life church, the call for relation ship does not end with those within the church it extends to relationship with the greater community. Including, offering backpacks for kids in need, blood drives with the Red Cross or Christmas dinners organized for the local veterans counseling office. A Christian focused recovery group called Celebrate Recovery met every week to provide a faith affirming focus to any 'life possessor' whether it be alcohol, drugs or other addictions.

This is the community focused ideology that guided Jack's vision into fruition in his early years. "It's funny to think that when you really look at it, the focus of many Churches is not about their communities. They want you inside their walls but they don't encourage members to go outside the walls to the local mission field (the local community)." In Jack's mission he has been encouraged by several different pastors to develop leadership and evangelism all stemming from 'relational evangelism.'

Jack's passion for people encouraged him to look for opportunities to share God's love outside of church programs. He found this in a volunteering opportunity in the local school system in which, he formerly worked at so many years ago. Jack participated in the "Peer Mentoring" program. The program is designed by guidance counselors to assist students whom they see in need of social advocacy. "He was a good kid but you could see he had a target on his back. He didn't have a dad, his mother was busy at work, didn't have many friends in school. He was picked on a lot." For one study hall session every week Jack would meet with the student to play chess. He would ask how the student was doing, and show him new chess moves, but Jack's favorite thing to do, as anyone who's met him will attest, was just to try and make him laugh.

"God doesn't need you to say his name all the time. Most of the time He simply wants you!" Jack was not allowed to be in contact with the student outside of the scheduled hours. He was not allowed to speak about religion and nor did he want to. His role was simply to offer relief and refuge from whatever the day was bringing.

After eight years Jack was seeing the fruits of his labor blossom into his vision of a community build on grace and relationship with The Holy Spirit. He had become known not simply as seasoned minister, but as a cherished part of the local community. His heart had informed his words and throughout all the various challenges Jack felt God's hand guiding him. From the wheelchair he had risen to stand every Sunday and speak of the love and devotion of Jesus Christ. The money problems sorted themselves out, his family remained by his side, and those who had been frazzled by his decision to pursue his dreams now stood in awe. By all accounts, Jack was seeing his trust in God reaffirmed time and time again. Yet, one thing was nagging at Jack's heart. After, making a promise to himself to never limit his dreams due to fear, he had one more mountain to climb, or actually to jump off. Finally, at the age of 53, he would take the leap. Literally, to celebrate his 53rd birthday he felt the joy and exhilaration of free falling from high above the earth on a skydiving trip. Everything in his life appeared to be unfolding like a story book. His family of five was blossoming. The church he planted with a handful of people was now established and flourishing. But the test of faith which Jack never saw coming, was around the life's next bend in the road. Jack's life and the life of his family would never be same following the morning of September 20th, 2018.

TRAGEDY

In the middle of September the warm breeze of summer began to lift. A New England autumn was announcing it's presence as it fell the leaves from their branches and began it's cold whispers of a winter to come. A time during which the common case cold or a flu is certainly no cause for alarm in the average New Englander. Jack had become feverish, congested and felt an aching in his muscles. While discomforting, it appeared to be nothing a few tablets and plenty of liquids couldn't take care of. The second day felt very much the same, though Jack complained of a bit more discomfort. Megan stayed home to keep an eye on him. He was notably weakened by this supposed flu, but nothing about this felt entirely dangerous. The regiment of liquids, vitamins and naps continued.

The third day however brought severe suspicions that something more was wrong. Again, working from home to nurse her husband, Megan noticed Jack didn't seem like himself. He began to stand up and walk around with no real indication of where he was going or what he was going to do. His balance seemed disoriented, peculiar since he had designed this house with ease of access in mind and knew every corner. But even stranger was his silence.

Megan became concerned and felt his feverish symptoms might have been tiring him. She decided to put Jack to bed and hope his head cleared in the morning.

At three in the morning an incredible shriek and shout was heard. Megan turned over in her bed to see Jack grunting and groaning. "Jack, Jack!" She pressed her arms against him, an attempt to wake him from a possible nightmare. Still Jack screamed and murmured. Megan noticed his eyes were not shut but open. "Jack, what's wrong?" "My arm!" Jack shouted. Megan was taken aback. The comment made no sense. The door opened and their daughter Maddy came into the room, awakened by the sudden disturbance. "What's wrong with Dad?" She asked.

Jack was feral. He writhed and howled but with no ability to comprehend his struggle. "I don't know." Megan responded. She quickly picked up her phone and dialed two of Jack's closest friends, Mike and Paul. Within minutes they were there and helped load Jack into a car to bring him to the hospital. Lost in his incomprehensive state, Jack could not remember his lifelong friends. He became irritable and confused.

When they arrived at the emergency room Jack was asked what was wrong and he claimed again it was his arm. Why was he here? Who were all these people? "Megan, Megan what're they doing?" Of everything in the haze of his delusion, the face of his wife was the only thing he could cling to.

Ushered into a cramped Emergency Waiting area, EMTs and physicians began their inquiries. They took blood tests, tested his faculties and continued to struggle against Jack's resistant confusion. Alongside Jack, Megan too was lost in a sea of chaos. Rampant questions lead to uncertain answers in repetition. As they awaited test results so they could start some type of treatment and take a step in the right direction, Maddy did her best to comfort her father while Megan made phone calls to the family. Jon came down from the mountains of Vermont and Hannah from the city of Philadelphia. Each had a four hour drive to Connecticut. By the time they arrived, Jack had been in the emergency room for over eight hours. The physicians had also just come back with the bloodwork. Suicide was being questioned. Outrageous, how could such a thing be said? A strong amount of acetaminophen had been found in Jack's blood levels. The abuse of headache medicines can cause kidney failure and is often an indication of suicide by pharmacy. Impossible, Jack would never. Megan pondered the excessive amounts Jack had been taking over the past few days.

With Jack's kidney's failing, his blood flow began to stagnate and oxygen levels were becoming low. There was now a worry that his heart may be next to fail. Citing the possibility of poisoned blood, an infectious disease specialist named Doctor Lawler was called in. This old and certain man, whose knowledge came not just from his diploma but from the sweat on his smock, declared it was "sepsis."

Jack was put on support systems, intubated through his throat to provide air flow and given several IV's for vitals, then transferred to the Intensive Care Unit. More tests needed to be conducted. MRIs and CT scans would be conducted to see if brain activity was affected by the bad blood coursing through his veins. In the waiting room his family sat with a disturbance in their hearts as they pondered "Where could this have come from?" Dr. Lawler informed them that the infection of the blood or other tissues that caused Sepsis, could have come from anywhere, since these bacteria often live on the surface of our skin. But if introduced into the bloodstream, it can present serious damages to vital organs, induce shock and possibly death. Where it came from was not important at the moment, the priority was to stop it.

The first solid answer came with partial relief but greater fear. This was not guesswork anymore. This indeed was a battle with Sepsis. As Jack underwent his tests, his family sat with their difficult questions and answers. Chaos had erupted into their lives but here they stood together. When they were finally permitted to see Jack, they took immediate occupation of his room. Though intubated and sedated, though no word could be spoken; upon the sight of his children through the haze of his septic shock Jack's eyes gleamed. An immediate tear and dilation of the pupil told his family just what they needed to know; Jack knew they were there.

They spent the night by his side and in the second day there came a new concern about his blood pressure. It had been confirmed that the infection had reached Jack's heart. A physician commented that further procedures would require a statement of DNR (Do Not Resuscitate). If Jack were to lose stability during surgery there was no guaranteed outcome for his quality of life. MRI and CT scans had confirmed the infected blood had reached the brain and minimal wavelengths were being registered. Further disturbance could put them into a permanent imbalance.

The family's first breath of air tasted bitter, dry and strangely cold for a late day in September. After forty-eight hours of cramped corridors, rampant questions, the smell of bleach, and all that beeping...what would've been a welcome moment of reprieve, was instead brought the incredible angst of life and death. Thoughts of what has become, what lay beyond, what could be done continued to swirl in their heads. Their tears of distress attested to the fact that they dreaded having to have any say in the matter, but one thing was for certain. Despite the cautions of the medical staff, something told them that in the end this outcome wouldn't be in their hands. That Jack would get better. That Jack would walk out of this hospital and come home. And they would be there every step of the way.

Over the next five days, blood tests were continuously run. Jack was monitored in the ICU, but now also quarantined in his room. To protect him from further infection, there were standards and procedures put in place to keep him stable. Visitations were limited to one or two people at a time. Either Maddy, Hannah, Jon or Megan stayed consistently by his side, each wrapped in a protective gown and surgical mask. At night, one of the kids would stay and keep watch over Jack while the others got what sleep they could in their own beds. Megan and Maddy often shared a bed. Her daughter's presence warmed the creased indent left in the mattress by Jack's absence from Megan's side.

The house became a center of operation. Meals and lunches were pre-packed, schedules made around the visitation hours, family members were picked up and escorted to see what they could allow of Jack. "My kids became my strength." Megan says of those days. "I felt scared. But each hour I grew strangely more peaceful.

My family felt like a shield from the darkness." Maddy balanced her school hours with visiting hours, Hannah had recently graduated from Philadelphia University as a Physician's Assistant and was awaiting her employment at Hartford Hospital in their Neurosurgery department. Like Jon, she had packed up her things to return home for an indefinite stay. The entire family was under one roof again, each leaving their own established lives to come home and protect the core of the life they had always known.

Megan worked in the adjacent hospital wing of the Children's Medical Center and was familiar with the procedural routines. She often found herself asking many questions of the physicians and she carefully wrote down each detail in her notebook. Having her own medical knowledge, she was able to find some comfort in her ability to at least understand the situation. Being able to compartmentalize, she found herself able to hide her emotions and stave off worry. She was persistent in her search for answers. If the doctors couldn't figure it out, maybe she could by asking the right questions. Maybe she could help.

One night a nurse came by and told her she could go home. Megan said she would, but would be right back. The Nurse teasingly said "Oh, you're one of those." The comment resonated with Megan as true. Sure enough, each day Megan would orchestrate the family's schedule with its various meetings, visits and household affairs while they awaited further news of Jack's tests and a plan of action.

Now a week into his stay at the hospital, Jack was finally

stabilized enough to be moved from Intensive Care into the Step-Down Unit. Here Jack would be further monitored and prepared for the upcoming surgeries. Jack was now stable, he was able to be taken off intubation. For the first time in a week, he could speak. A sense of joy fluttered through the room. The family huddled around Jack, he was able to look into each of their eyes and sound out their names. He started to make jokes and funny faces to try and get the room to laugh. But Jack was still not Jack. Though stable and able to use his vital organs, Jack's brain was still affected. His mental faculties had not returned in full. His blood flow was still poisoned and struggling to produce ample supply to his brain. It was decided that heart surgery would be necessary. The sepsis had eaten away at one of his heart valves and it would need to be replaced. Doctor Lawler introduced a cardiothoracic surgeon named Doctor Cheema, a man of concise intellect and phrasing. He put forth no other option than immediate surgery. Jack would be given two days to rest and then be taken in.

The following days were a mixture of impatience and relief. Fear had not fully subsided, since the mortality rate of an open heart surgery under such a condition is 40%. But although Jack was incoherent, the eyes of his family recognized his subtle smiles and eye contact that came not from his body, but his soul. It was strange for the nurses to often hear the laughter that came from his family in the Step-Down Unit. Like many patients who shared this floor, Jack was far from out of the woods. But throughout those days, his family insisted on seeing him and listening to him speak. Though incoherent, not remembering or fully communicative; he was there. They could see it, even if others could not. The doctors had to stop further infection, Jack's blood needed to be replaced. Through a process of plasmolysis, his blood would slowly be replaced over the next few days. On the first Saturday of October, two days later, Jack was sent in for open heart surgery. The family came in the early morning hours to go to Jack's room and walked with him every step of the way toward the large swinging doors that read "Surgery Personnel Only." And then they waited. At the suggestion of Doctor Cheema, the family returned home to find some reprieve, and the hospital said they would call them when Jack's surgery concluded. Jon, one never good with sitting still, took a walk in the local forest. Hannah and Maddy distracted themselves with their hometown seasonal Apple Harvest Festival. Megan did not leave the hospital. She listened to worship music, called her family with updates and tried to distract herself with noteworthy tasks.

The call came four hours later and announced Jack was out of surgery. The family raced to the hospital to meet him. Doctor Cheema greeted the family and declared that he had just replaced one of the most damaged heart valves he's ever seen. Jack's heart was stable and had been implanted with a pig valve replacement.

He was waiting in the recovery wing where the family would be able to see him.

They arrived in the now fourth foreign room Jack had been relocated to and rushed to his side. Though not conscious, there was a look of peace to Jack as he slumbered. Despite several I.V drips, Jack appeared to be breathing on his own and some color had returned to his face. Doctor Cheema advised that Jack would most likely be out of consciousness for a day or so but indicated that he did not suspect any brain damage had occurred. Doctor Cheema further advised that the family take the next few days to have their own period of recovery for when Jack woke up. There was still a lot to consider and challenges ahead for his recovery.

Following the surgery Jack was put back into the ICU. He was not very responsive or communicative. The family would take shifts by his side, watching his eyes for signs of returning life. It was a thankful moment when he was extubated sooner than predicted, which meant his body was able to provide its own air flow. The family followed Jack through the halls over the next day as he was transferred from the ICU to Step Down to the Cardiac Floor where he was finally settled for surgical recovery with another patient. Jack was alive, but as the family members would shift in and out throughout the days, it became somewhat difficult to gauge if Jack was communicating. Though his body was responding well physically, his mind was still assembling itself and Doctors warned it would take time.

A few days later, at three O'clock in the morning, Megan received a phone call. "Megan! You've got to come get me! I'm in Texas!" Baffled, Megan wondered if she was still in a dream. "Jack?" She asked. "Megan where am I?" Jack's voice called out from the unrecognized phone number. "I can't find my phone." Jack declared. Megan leapt out of her bed and woke the family. Jack was up, he just called her! Their footsteps pounded the floor as they raced out of the house and into the car toward the hospital.

HERE WE GO, AGAIN

The scene was surreal, a dream trapped in waking thoughts. Beeping machines, tubes lining his body, white sanitary walls and people with masks all around him. A corded phone hung off his bed, still beeping from a dropped call. "Sir, please stop moving. Hartford Hospital, you're in Hartford hospital." A pair of eyes shimmered in the dark, their hands commanded his sore body. His legs. "Why can't I feel my legs?" Jack asked. "You need to relax, take a deep breath." "Where..."

Suddenly the door opened, all in the room turned to see a woman holding several bags, appropriately smocked and guarded with a face mask. But her eyes, there was no mistaking those eyes. "Megan." Jack called out. She rushed toward him. Behind her trailed three more dressed just like her in a mixture of pajamas and medical garb, "Hannah, Jonathan, Maddy! What...what're you doing here?" He asked. The confusion swam in his eyes, nurses carried out their routines. "It's okay, Jack. You're going to be okay." Megan whispered as she clutched his hand and soothed his chaotic gaze. "Everything is going to be okay."

The following day Doctor Lawler and Cheema were alerted that Jack had woken up. They came into the room at morning to explain all that was happening with the sepsis, his kidneys, the heart valve. Jack was safe now but he had a good two years estimated recovery, a long road ahead of him. "It was strange, over those first few days, I don't think I fully comprehended much beyond the fact that I was in the hospital for my heart. But it didn't scare me. I'd been in the hospital thirty years before, I'd lost the use of my legs before. But eventually I got them back. God gave them back, I believed he'd give me my life back too." Jack says of his faith in the face of his terror.

The experience of '82 ushered in some de ja vu for Jack. Just as before, his legs and muscles had greatly deteriorated and he would require rehabilitation assistance to learn how to walk, eat and fulfill other occupations. Jack would not be returning home yet. While the hospital could discharge him, his condition required a facility that could maintain his daily routines. Again, the family drew up their plans, someone would stay with Jack while the others would run errands, and Megan would begin looking around for a rehabilitation facility for Jack.

Megan found that many facilities were no better than the hospitals. Three to four to a room, cramped quarters, a high volume of patients. In more places than not, it felt like a step backward for Jack. While these were qualified medical facilities, there was concern that a possible six month stay would consort some misery and he would not be receiving the critical attention required. Many of the patients were short term, and their routines required less attention or therapeutic aggressions. Following some less than pleasant site visitations, Megan made a phone call to the Hartford Hospital Patient Rehabilitation Director. She inquired about any possible suggestion for facility and was answered with a saving grace. Hartford Hospital had just opened up a new rehabilitation wing and had an open bed. After some additional inquiry, a decision was made that Jack would be able to extend his stay with Hartford Hospital in the new wing. Jack would not only retain the resources of his doctors, but would be attended to by a full team of therapy professionals and all only a stone's throw away from Megan's office on the other side of campus.

Jack's room was a single suite with a bedside window, a television and a personal bathroom. All outfitted with the necessary medical assistances required. While out of surgery, Jack's blood required continuous tests and there was still the worry of the need to monitor brain activity. While restored to coherence, Jack's brain had still suffered some mild damage that would need to be rehabilitated through cognitive and physical therapies. A speech therapist was assigned to restore his ability to communicate, a physical therapist to assist in restoration of his muscle functions, and a vocational therapist to help reassimilate his daily routines.

His days became a routine of exercise, therapies, tests and blood samples. CAT scans and MRIs were conducted around the clock, sometimes waking him in the early morning. During these days Jack remained as active as possible. In times of rest he would often welcome visitors, members of the church and family who were finally permitted to come to see him. When Megan, Hannah, Maddy or Jon could spare a moment they were instantaneously by his bedside with warm food or a beloved copy of Jack's favorite movie Rocky. The room of the rehabilitation wing was filled with good spirits. Jack was making progress. "Even though I felt every day, being hoisted up and asked to stand but not being able to, I felt that I knew I could do it, but I was also a bit disappointed it wasn't happening as quickly. I wasn't eighteen anymore, my body wasn't recovering like it had." While the nurses and therapists would cheer Jack on and say "Look! You're walking!" He knew he was not. But he kept in good faith, and he spoke with friends and family often reaffirming his belief that sometime soon he would walk out that door again.

However, complications would arise following a routine scan one day. A dark shadow had been spotted on Jack's right kidney and it was feared that a cancer tumor had grown. He was taken in for further testing immediately and suspicions were confirmed, about one-third of his kidney was infected. Surgery would have to take place. But first Jack had to recover from the trauma of Sepsis.

He had survived a 40% chance of dying from heart surgery, a stroke in his brain and nerve damage to his right leg which again challenged his ability to ever walk again. The news of cancer from the kidney specialist didn't terrify Jack. What would normally cause terror to arise in one's mind, Jack rehearsed and meditated on the miracles and of God's purpose for his life that could not be stopped. The doctors were not certain of the extent of the kidney cancer at this time but were all in agreement that kidney surgery could wait a few months. Jack was granted a three month reprieve on the procedure, and it was pushed from November 2018 to February 2019. But in the meantime, he would require continuous monitoring and blood work in addition to his rehabilitation.

"I was overwhelmed. As if I'd asked, 'what next?' and then BOOM." But Jack knew he would make it through. He often thought of the former visitation of God's presence through the green light when he was a teenager, the strength and courage he felt then. While it had not appeared by his bedside this time, he felt the glow of the Holy Spirit within his heart. Jack was told if he kept up with the progress he was making, he could take a day trip to visit his home, a place he had not known in well over a month now. With this prospect, Jack became inspired. His therapies were aggressive, even though each small step took tremendous strength. The feeling in his legs progressed, although it took all of his strength and frustrated his pride, his foot now raised an inch off the ground, and eventually he was able to pull himself off the bed. Feats that nearly three weeks ago would've been impossible. The two to four weeks of rehabilitation felt like an eternity. Each day Jack would be pushed to his limits, his legs, muscles and heart challenged to return full function. "Always look for movement, they said. That's how you know you're recovering. If you don't see movement, it...can get discouraging." The therapists carried their duties of nurturing and pushing Jack in his exercises, each time demanding he take that next step even if he couldn't. The hours were long and often left him exhausted at the end of the day. When not sharing a home cooked meal over his lunch tray with his family or visiting with a church member, he often found himself in times of reflection regarding this new life journey. "I would just look up, remember that green light and say 'okay, you've done it before, you'll do it again." Jack's outlook always remained positive. Reinforced by his faith, his family, and his efforts he knew he would walk out of the hospital again and return home. A week before Jack's discharge date, he received a welcome surprise.

Today, he would be taking a scouting trip to his house. The physical Therapist would be looking at his home to make recommendations on required accommodations to enable Jack to return home. Megan and the family would be on their way over soon to bring him to the house. He made ready, with some assistance from his attending nurse, and he was soon whisked away into a wheelchair and down the elevator. The doors slid open, a crowd of people buzzed in the lobby, forward Jack went. The entrance doors opened, a breeze brushed in to touch his face, and outside a familiar white SUV was waiting to take him away. "Home."

Jon drove the SUV slowly and cracked the windows, it was a warm autumn day and Jack had taken to the front seat. His eyes watched the window, lost as they would be in youth on an unfamiliar road trip, taking in the unknown and unremembered. Megan, Maddy and Hannah sat in the backseat. Each smiled and petted at Jack's arm when they asked him "How're you feeling?" To which he would respond "I can't believe it." The turning leaves fluttered about, colors and cars glided past as if they were old friends. And then came the driveway and those two familiar pillars, supporting a roof over a walking   path leading out to the driveway where three vehicles were parked. The Subaru from Vermont, the SUV from Philadelphia and Jack's favorite truck. They pulled into the drive and opened the door. "Welcome back dad." His daughters said as they escorted him from the car into the house. Another car followed shortly behind and pulled in to the drive, it was the therapists arriving and they announced they could take their time but that they would begin their examinations shortly.

With his walker Jack moved about slowly with a crowd of four hovering, watching his every move. His eyes scanned the house in reverence, as he explained each detail to both of the therapists. "The bedroom is over there, I used to have a wall here but I knocked it down so I could move around easier. I knew I'd be getting old so every thing's on the first floor. I put my bathroom close to my bed, with a high seat, oh and there's the fireplace. I like to sit there in the winter." The home had been remodeled just a year ago from the frame out to give Megan, the home that she had dreamed of. Walls had been moved and removed. She finally had a dream kitchen. Yet, this house also had a prophetic design. He had built a house that would only require one step to live comfortably with his aging difficulties. The therapists and family watched Jack, each taking notes on where steps, handles and other assistance could be necessary. He wandered his home absorbing every fine detail of it until finally growing tired, he sat on the couch where he began to cry. "I can't believe it."

The family and therapists gathered in empathy, these were not tears of sorrow but relief. "I know how you feel right now, but we're going to have to take you back for a few more days." One of them finally broached. "Of course, just five more minutes." Jack asked. The therapists obliged and for a few moments Jack sat surrounded by his family and home. Each sharing a brief thanks and cry of relief for having made it this far.

ALIVE IN HIS PURPOSE

Two weeks later Jack was returned home for good. His family had made ample preparations and a series of appointments were put on the calendar for Jack to continue his out-patient recovery. While the kidney surgery was nearing, Jack was returning just in time for the holidays. Three weeks later, Jack miraculously would spend Thanksgiving with his family. To say they were thankful would be a gross understatement. It was decided to further postpone the surgery until after the new year so Jack could gain his strength and return to his daily living. Though this routine would prove to be just as arduous as it was in the hospital. Bloodwork still had to be done, therapists would come by for inhouse visits in addendum to office visits, a regiment of prescriptions would have to be filled, and Jack needed supervision.

While Jack was able to move with a walker, often times his recovery was a tiring process. "It felt like I had a part time job. Be here, do this, take that. Every day, different times. But I knew it only meant I was getting better." The family worked continuously to maintain Jack's recovery efforts. Maddy served him breakfast and medication before going to school, Hannah sat with him until her afternoon shift at a new job as a Physicians Assistant at Hartford Hospital, working with some of the very doctors who had saved her father's life. Jon would provide lunch, give him rides to afternoon appointments before his evening shift at the supermarket and Megan would manage her client appointments with Jack's own to keep up and be at as many as possible. It was a tiring existence, but as time went on Jack's spirits and body gradually lifted.

The family's orchestrated efforts kept Jack's focus in good spirits and any spare moment was spent appreciating his return. In the coming Christmas, the whole family would receive a Christmas miracle as they united in celebration, for the second time in their lives Jack once again walked. A second miracle added to the countless blessings. In each opening grace, Jack's name was called out in thanksgiving. During this Christmas, Jack returned to the place that God had called him to all those years ago.

Jack's kidney cancer was a growing concern and he was finally stable enough to go in for surgery. "I wasn't really that scared, I thought well after all I've just been through I'm still here. People donate kidneys all the time and I've still got two." Once again, a few weeks into the new year, February of 2019, five months after Sepsis and open heart surgery; Jack returned to the hospital with his family and he was ushered into the operating room for a second time. Though this stay would be brief, a mere six hours after surgery, they were informed the whole kidney had to be removed. The cancer had grown and rather than orthoscopic surgery they had to cut in through the abdomen to remove the whole kidney. Jack would recover over the next two days before again being discharged, a breeze compared to his prior three months stay but with this new development came some setbacks in his overall recovery.

The surgery had left a large six inch scar along the center of his stomach, what muscles he retained were quick to atrophy and now having his one kidney would require even more diligence and monitoring of his blood work. "It was a bit disappointing, I felt like I had taken two steps back. I had gotten so far, but now I felt like I was back to where I was. But, at least they were letting me leave the hospital this time.

Jack's recovery routines continued for the next six months. Exercise five days a week, appointments every other, new needle marks from required blood monitoring during every visit. Medications were adjusted, prescribed, unprescribed. Under the incredible persistence of his medical regimen, Jack eventually regained mobility and was able to drive himself. Often, he would take a ride to go and sit down by the nearby river or spend what time he could at the church and return to speaking every Sunday. Jack was beginning to pick up the pieces.

In October Jack's friends from the church invited him to a concert. At good standing in his recovery, Jack had recently graduated from a walker to a cane and he decided they would attend. Together, he and Megan went with their friends to enjoy their night out. But while the show was alive with music and cheer, Jack became perturbed as the night progressed. A growing sensation of swelling grew within. His feet, his hands, his arms and chest all suddenly began to feel tight against his clothes. All at an alarmingly rapid pace. His body was stiffening as he walked to the restroom during the concert. Jack stumbled and fell to his knees before being able to get upright and arrive at the restroom.

A few days following the concert his swelling worsened, his body was retaining water weight and what had been 185lb at the start of the week was now at 225lb. His face looked bloated, his body swollen and he knew something was wrong. "I felt weaker and weaker." After a consultation with his kidney doctor it was decided to check Jack back into the hospital where further examination found that his one remaining kidney was being overwhelmed and toxic waste was not leaving his body. Had they brought him in any later his kidney would have become fully destroyed and would've required dialysis. It was decided to boost the kidney function with a steroid agent called Prednisone, which would help the kidney maintain its functions. The hospital would also hold Jack for another fourteen days, and once again, prayer resumed, "Lord, cause this remaining kidney to function."

Jack was ushered back into the confines of Hartford Hospital, but unlike his previous stay, he shared a room with one other patient. "Thinking I would be there only a few days, I let the other person take what I call the window seat. That three days turned out to be 16!" "Here I am again," Jack thought, while he retained some good spirit towards getting through this, the constant drain, the back and forth, better than worse, was all beginning to wear on him. The patient who shared a bed across from him and could not swallow. Frequently in the middle of the night, Jack was awakened by frightening gasps and choking to which would cause nurses to proceed to vacuum out the patient's throat. "I felt so awful, he was in such suffering. I prayed every night that he would find some sort of relief. I was sure he was going to die." During the sixteen days, Jack was often scanned and prodded for bloodwork, around the clock every three hours, whether awake or not. Amidst the grief and angst of the fellow patients, a nurse's aid appeared and offered to wash his feet. "She struck me. Here was this seventy year old woman who does this every day, every day she sees such grief, anger, pain and every day she comes to wash our feet. It was like a biblical scene, her sense of grace." In conversation, Jack began to talk about his faith with this compassionate caretaker. "I tried to be a light" during those two weeks while facing great disappointments and challenges. Jack felt affirmed that not only was he going to get through this, God was going to use all of it for His purpose.

Upon the completion of these 16 days in the hospital, Jack again returned home. His routines were now balancing his heart, kidney and muscle functions. Therapies remained in place and after about a month Jack once again returned to the state where he could drive and walk with his cane. Each step repeated just as painful as the last, but at least back to where he was. His activities at the church resumed and life was again starting to reassemble.

On a cold winter day, five or so weeks his recovery from the failure of his remaining kidney, Jack was walking through a parking lot when he felt a sharp pain in his right leg. He was halfway to his car and near collapse. He could not move another inch. By God's grace, a passerby saw him in pain and offered to get him to his car. Feeling a throbbing pain in his right leg, Jack grit his teeth drove home and had Megan make phone calls to the kidney MD. After a series of tests it was determined that the Prednisone steroid that had been prescribed had eaten way the cartilage in Jack's right hip ball. A common side effect of the drug. It was decided that surgery would take place to replace the hip with an artificial one and

Jack would have to cease his rehabilitations until then to further prevent damage. The date was set for a few weeks away in July.

Trapped in the limbo of a worldwide lock down due to the arrival of the COVID-19 pandemic, Jack waited out the following weeks with only a painkiller subscription to quell his ever growing pains. He was returned not just to limited mobility, but to a place where access to medical necessities became challenging. Appointments were canceled, prescriptions sparse and his operation on temporary hiatus. Like much of the world, he was again restrained to a room. The nights became painful and the swelling remained a constant concern. He tried to get what exercise he could but without access to facilities or staff, his progress remained very much halted and his pain was continual though managed. As the reality of Covid masked hysteria settled over the world, the days passed slowly, yet, eventually a call came in July that Jack's surgery would be able to proceed under the new COVID-19 standards. Jack was brought into the hospital only to be released twenty-four hours later with a titanium hip in his right side. "It was incredible. Instantly I felt better, I mean I was sore. But I was thankful to just be sore. Most people's definition of 'pain' is just 'sore', but when you go through what surgeries I have 'sore' is a blessing."

His second surgery in six months had been a success, though

his rehabilitation had felt that step backward. Jack returned to using a walker and again had to be driven around for more appointments and more medications. After a near six months of waiting, Jack finally felt some relief. Following both the recovery of his body and the society at large under COVID-19, Jack was eventually able to return to his Physical Therapist appointments. But only a few days after returning to his exercise, the left side of his hip felt a familiar exhausting pain. Again, he returned to the hospital to find that the necessary steroid treatments had now eaten the left ball of his hip and would need to be replaced. For a fourth time, Jack went into the hospital to face a surgery, and again he shrugged saying "I know I'll get through this." The second hip replacement went without any further complication and the same relief was provided for the left side of his hip. Now with two new hips, one kidney, a new heart valve and a continuous regime of medications, Jack once again returned home. While some discomfort still prevailed, Jack's body underwent its recovery and rehabilitations through the remaining days without incident. After four major surgeries in the span of two years, only a year of being home and every day that was a struggle in between, Jack finally was able to see an end. He had made it through. The pieces, while put together differently now, had all been picked up.

As if the strain and discomfort from multiple surgeries, the rehabilitation required to walk without having a feeling or sensation in his right leg, adjusting to life with kidney dysfunction and rehabilitating from two hip replacements weren't enough. The news that brought the most devastation to Jack's life was the discovery of a non-cancerous tumor that was growing in Megan's brain. A benign brain tumor had been discovered in Megan's brain and needed to be removed as soon as possible. Plans had been in place since March of 2020. "I could by God's grace, deal with my own pain and disabilities, but to see my wife go through this was the proverbial straw that broke the camel's back. I was overwhelmed, I was in desperate need of God's presence." Thankful, Megan's family including her dad, mom, sister and niece flew in from Washington State to help care for Jack and Megan as they simultaneously recovered from these major surgeries.

Jack was once again able to drive and began returning to his work at the church on a regular basis. Some Oasis members had left during his own absence, the pandemic had further drawn people away but every Sunday, Jack would return to stand at the pulpit and tell of his blessings. Beside him, his family too saw a light at the end of their tunnel. What each had been asked to forfeit for the last two years, each returned to; Maddy graduated college, Hannah pursued a career opportunity in the very hospital that had been her father's home for many weeks over the past two years, and she also became engaged, Jon moved back to his home in Vermont. Megan returned to work. Although life was different now, she and Jack had new priorities. Being driven by church and work responsibilities no longer took precedence in their lives. They would endeavor to rest in the knowledge that God had shown himself faithful in bringing them both through the storms of the previous three years.

In many ways these seasons of tribulation, faith proved challenging but within each person a much greater connection grew with the grace of what it means to witness a miracle. "If life wasn't in perspective before, it certainly is now." Jack often stated. As time went on Jack's blood work halted, prescriptions became less, and appointments were less frequent. To this day, Jack remains diligent with his rehabilitation and still frequents a physical therapist. "I think that's the hardest part. Accepting it's never over. There's no 'normal' to go back to. This is it. This is my life now." Jack speaks often to many with a glimmer in his eye and a cane in his hand. "I knew that the Lord had a plan. Knew it all along. But that's always easiest said than done."

Recovery is a long process. It takes the mind, spirit and body. While Jack acknowledges his life has its challenges. "It's time, that's what makes it so hard. Throughout my entire stay at the hospital I would swear it was next week I'd get out only to find

I had another four weeks. Even now, when I'm out I sometimes think 'man, do I have to go back yet?' and who knows if I ever will. Only time will tell. I just have to be happy to be alive. Sincerely."

Currently Jack has resumed full time duties of his church, the doors are once again open and he speaks from the pulpit most Sundays as he continues to share his heart to any who will listen. He walks with a cane but has lost over forty-five pounds after recovering from steroid treatment, his face gleams with a cherub's smile and his voice is as loud as ever when he tells a good joke. In frequent visits, his family often sits around and recalls how much has happened in through this three year journey. How in each of their lives, Jack was and remains a source of love and inspiration. The warm rays of sun glistening off Lake Champlain during Jack and Megan's frequent visits to Vermont while visiting Jon. God's promise remains faithful in allowing Jack and Megan to be a part of Hannah's wedding plans as she marries a new family member, the love of her life, Rourk. Maddy was excited to begin her transition to a new city and graduate school. The Chamis Family home remains a setting for Megan's wonderful cooking and friends. And amidst challenges, disappointments and uncertainty; Jack remains as cheerful as ever.

"I remember in the hospital one night praying, I said 'Lord, please...please just let me live long enough to see my children's weddings." Jack recalls. When asked what it was that carried him through these trying times, of life and death he has only one response. "Faith." Any numerous amounts of attempts could be taken to fully appreciate the miracles seen in Jack's life. For those who have seen it firsthand, it would be difficult to find the words to describe the incredible courage they saw in him during those hardships. How with every report, every setback he never once denounced himself or his belief that God would see him through. To account for such things in full description and anointing of such an experience deserves is an insurmountable task. But to any who will listen, Jack's story is as close as one could find fit to listen to the exploration of it. By faith and devotion, of tribulation and suffering; a persistent grace that any man could excuse under such extraordinary circumstances.

Early in his life Jack pledged his heart to the Lord, at certain times he feared he hadn't the heart at all. But he trusted his faith in God and felt it guide him. He raised a family, pursued his heart's call, founded a church, and remains of a staple of charity in his community to this day. Just as any life is faced with it's hardships, Jack has always maintained a positive outlook. His heart is reinforced by the love of Christ and the empowerment of the Holy Spirit that inspire him and keeps his thoughts in continual relation to the One he worships. He stands humble with his cane and his free hand reaches out to any who may need it. His eyes glisten in the sun whether winter or summer, his heart beats in renewed strength and his mouth sings to all who will listen "Hallelujah! Hallelujah!"

How is it that such joy can exist? How is it we find such affirmation in the face of peril? How is it we can learn to swing with such grace when life is in the balance? How is it that one can continue to live in the eye of an ever looming storm? As Jack will tell you "You gotta have faith." And for any who find themselves at the Oasis of Life Church, tucked away in the shopping plaza of Rocky Hill, CT know that your questions are one step closer to their answers as you listen to the message of Jack and his Seasons of Faith.

A WORD FROM JACK

I am aware, that looking at my life from the outside (as many have reminded me), seems far from ideal. My life has not been an easy one, yet it is full of blessing, truly, I am a blessed man. As I share my life story with so many, the question most commonly asked is why would God let this happen to you? Whenever tragedy strikes us or the world we live in, the question that is primarily asked, is; "Why, would a good God let bad things happen"? Especially in the life of a man or woman who has committed their life to serving Him. Saying, "I don't always know", seems like a side step. However, I do think it's the most honest answer I can offer.

Let me say, I don't believe God was the cause of my tragic accident at the age of 16 in 1982. I believe the primary cause was a group of teenage boys deciding that drinking beer all day at the beach and then driving at excessive speeds on the back roads of Connecticut was a good idea, this might be the cause leading to the effect. As Newton's third law states, "for every dumb teenage boy's action, there is a unfortunate Reaction!" I don't see God as the Cause, I seem Him as the saving Reaction to the cause. The Bible says, "that He will turn all things for good, for those who love God and follow in His ways". My prayer is that through reading this account of my life, that regardless of what you are facing, you too can believe that if we turn to God, He will turn even our failures into blessings.

It has been 40 years since that seemingly beautiful day on August, 14,1982. To say my life changed forever on that day would be a gross understatement. Actually, every detail of my life changed for me that day. I would never know again what it would mean to have a day where I would walk without struggle or discomfort. I would never again run to get somewhere or just for the fun of it. Never again, would I go anywhere without knowing exactly where the bathroom is located. Unfortunately, it took a few embarrassments to teach me this lesson. As hard as I've worked out at the gym, I've had to accept, that "there can be a will, but not always a way" to the road to complete recovery. I had to redefine what I thought it meant to be a "so called" man.

It was only when I finally, bowed my knee in surrender to my God and my Savior, Jesus Christ that I understood what it means to be a man and what the purpose of life truly is. I know, I know, you heard it all before, many have made the same claim and yet their lives look remarkably the same as the rest of humanity. I can only tell you my story. I can honestly say my life been transformed as I have traveled my journey following the path of the only true example of what a man or woman should be, "Jesus Christ".

I began my journey from a Quadra paraplegic at the age of 16 to miraculously walking again. Many have said to me, "you had such determination or faith, or both". Nothing disturbs me more, it is a grave injustice to all who haven't had the privilege of recovery. As if to say, "if you only wanted it more you could have recovered". I am well aware of the honor and responsibility I carry in being graced by God to walk again. I know that it is for His Glory and His Purpose that I have received this gift of Healing.

As I sit here today, a lot has changed since that day in August 1982, my life changed course dramatically in so many ways due to that tragic day. Due to my remaining physical limitations, I enrolled in college and began my 25 year career as a teacher. Never, ever, would have I found this path if I was not forced there due to a body that couldn't climb ladders or crawl under a car efficiently. Working with my hands and helping people was my passion, and becoming a Technology Education teacher was a great marriage of the two. God truly does turn all things for Good.

My life has been marked by major events periodically, many have brought heartache and pain. Yet, sometimes, the Lord has just straight out blessed me. Other than surrendering to Christ, the greatest blessing in my life was the day that a beautiful little red headed woman walked into my life. When Adam saw Eve in the Garden, he responded, "now at last, bone of my bone and flesh of my flesh". My marriage to Megan Wheeler has blessed my life in every way "body, mind and spirit". She literally is the only woman in the world for me. Without her, I really would not be here to write these words. The fruit of this relationship is our three children, Jonathan Michael (author of this book), Hannah & Maddy. I am still in awe that my life has turned out so blessed. Who would have thought laying there paralyzed from the neck down unable to feel even the slightest touch or to lift a finger, that today I would have a life such as this. It was unimaginable that day in 1982. It was almost 35 years from that day in 1982 to September, 2018. In those 35 years, I had adjusted to life. I did not walk as well as others, but I walked. I was not as physically strong as most men, yet spiritually stronger than most. The difficulties of life have actually given me an unforeseen advantage. I've found that a life lived literally dependent on God is richer and more stable than a life which is established on self reliance. Many of us are aware of the parable of Jesus encouraging us, "to build our house (lives) on the Rock (Jesus).

Thankfully, Megan and I took the parable of Jesus to heart. We built a life that is established and developed by our faith and dependency upon our relationship with Jesus Christ. Every major life decision is governed by how it would ultimately benefit the kingdom of God. The parable in the Gospel of Matthew continues, "And the rain fell, and the floods came, and the winds blew and beat on that house, but it did not fall". Megan and I can state emphatically that if it were not for the Grace and empowerment of The Holy Spirit our house would have fallen. There are seasons in life (you might be there currently) where only the supernatural intervention of God can sustain your "body, mind and Spirit". In these seasons, it's not due to our strength that we make it through, but in spite of our weakness, God sustains us. It is in these seasons that we learn what true reliance upon God really means. It is in these seasons, that true empathy and compassion is nurtured in our lives. As the Psalmist states, "when my heart is overwhelmed lead me to the Rock that is higher than I".

We all ask, "what is the purpose of Life? ". I humbly submit, that the purpose is to learn the heart of our Father God, displayed in the life of Jesus Christ and lived out by the empowerment of His Holy Spirit. However, I don't believe the revelation will come by reading a book (not even this book), it must be lived out in every human beings' life journey. This book and a thousand like it, simply encourage many pilgrims to continue on their journey toward dependency upon God.

My prayer is that reading this book has inspired you to keep going on your journey with God or to begin a new journey with Him. A simple word of encouragement, the Bible says in the Gospel of John, "For God so loved the world, that he gave his only Son, that

whosever believes in Him will not perish but have eternal life."
Simply, ask Him, "Lord I need You, I don't want to go it alone".

Love, Jack & Megan Chamis

Made in the USA
Las Vegas, NV
09 October 2022

56802257R10069